Native Plant
GARDENING FOR
BIRDS, BEES & BUTTERFLIES

Upper Midwest

Jaret Daniels

Adventure Publications
Cambridge, Minnesota

DEDICATION

To my wife, Stephanie, for her unconditional love and support. I am continuously grateful to have such an amazing person with whom to share my life.

ACKNOWLEDGMENTS

Thanks to my parents for their enduring encouragement of my interest in natural history and all things wild.

Cover and book design by Lora Westberg and Jonathan Norberg
Edited by Brett Ortler
Proofread by Dan Downing

Photo credits:
Front cover: Anise Hyssop by **JurateBuiviene/shutterstock.com;** Ruby-throated hummingbird by **FotoRequest/shutterstock.com;** birdhouses by **picsbyst/shutterstock.com;** Showy Milkweed by **Michael Schober/shutterstock.com;** hummingbird background by **Vaclav Sebek/shutterstock.com;** Purple Coneflowers by **Barbara Wheeler/shutterstock.com**

Back cover: Nodding Onion by **Gerry Bishop/shutterstock.com;** Black-eyed Susans by **Quang Ho/shutterstock.com;** bumble bee by **kzww/shutterstock.com;** Common Buckeye by **Leena Robinson/shutterstock.com;** magnificent hummingbird male perched by **Stan Tekiela**

All photos by Jaret Daniels unless otherwise noted.

All photos copyright of their respective photographers. Some photos identified by page in a left (ex. L1) to right (ex. R1) order, descending. **Kelly Colgan Azar:** 40; **Travis Bonovsky:** 101; **Dave Czoschke:** 229; **Ellen M Falbowski:** 119; **Molly Fifield-Murray:** 79; **Michael Head:** 243; **Keith Kanoti, Maine Forest Service, Bugwood.org:** 155; **Diane Larson:** 115; **Matt Lavin:** 129, 142; **Brett Ortler:** 23; **Bron Praslicka:** 113; **Corey Raimond:** 225; **Dave Rogers:** 185; **Rob Routledge, Sault College, Bugwood.org:** 32 (L8), 169, 237 (Bigleaf Aster), 239; **Shelley Selle:** 73; **Steve Law at Brighton Plants:** 26 (R10), 118, 263 (5); **Stan Tekiela:** 269; **Peter Voigt:** 236 (Purple Milkweed), 246; **Michael Weatherford:** 191; **Alan Wells:** 165, 195

This image is licensed under the Attribution 3.0 Unported (CC BY 3.0) license, which is available at https://creativecommons.org/licenses/by/3.0/deed.en: **DDennisM:** 141

These images are licensed under the Attribution 2.0 Generic (CC BY 2.0) license, which is available at https://creativecommons.org/licenses/by/2.0/: **Judy Gallagher:** 245; **Kathy (rittysdigiez):** 209; **Fyn Kynd:** 215; **Carl Lewis:** 111; **Doug McGrady:** 89, 238; **OkaWenNF:** 139; **Kristine Paulus:** 145; **Bob Peterson:** 21 (bottom 6); **Andy Reago & Chrissy McClarren:** 203; **Shawn Taylor:** 173

These images are licensed under the CC0 1.0 Universal (CC0 1.0) Public Domain Dedication license, which is available at https://creativecommons.org/publicdomain/zero/1.0/or licensed under Public Domain Mark 1.0, which is available at https://creativecommons.org/publicdomain/mark/1.0/: **Doug Goldman, hosted by the USDA-NRCS PLANTS:** 34 (L2), 254; **Great Smoky Mountains National Park:** 61; **Haneesh KM.:** 272 (Indian Skipper larva); **karen_hine:** 71; **NC WETLANDS:** 199, 237 (False Nettle), 244; **USDA/Lance Cheung:** 227; **USDA NRCS Montana:** 28 (L6), 143

credits continued to page 275

10 9 8 7 6 5 4 3 2

Native Plant Gardening for Birds, Bees & Butterflies: Upper Midwest
Copyright © 2020 by Jaret Daniels
Published by Adventure Publications
An imprint of AdventureKEEN
310 Garfield Street South
Cambridge, Minnesota 55008
(800) 678-7006
www.adventurepublications.net
Printed in the United States of America
ISBN 978-1-59193-941-2 (pbk.); ISBN 978-1-59193-942-9 (ebook)

Table of Contents

Why You Should Plant a Garden

Once thought of as unattractive, weedy, or otherwise undesirable, native plants are growing in popularity nationwide. Much of this upsurge is due to the appeal of butterfly, bird, and pollinator gardening. Landscaping with native plants offers numerous benefits. First and foremost, it helps increase habitat and provides critical resources for wildlife. Studies have shown that including native plant species and increasing overall plant diversity, help support a greater abundance and diversity of wildlife. Natives are adapted to the growing conditions, such as soil and climate, of the locations where they naturally occur. As a result, they tend to perform better than non-native species once established, have fewer pest or disease problems, and require less water, fertilizer, and general maintenance—all of which can provide cost savings over time. Lastly, they add tremendous beauty to our landscapes and help provide increased opportunities for people to connect—or reconnect—with nature.

FIRST STEP: INVENTORY YOUR YARD

When you plant a garden, it's critical to select plants that will thrive on your property. This means considering a number of factors, such as light levels and soil conditions, but this isn't as complicated as it might seem at first. In fact, doing just a little homework ahead of time will improve your odds of growing healthy, beautiful plants—and attracting pollinators—dramatically.

CHECK YOUR HARDINESS ZONE

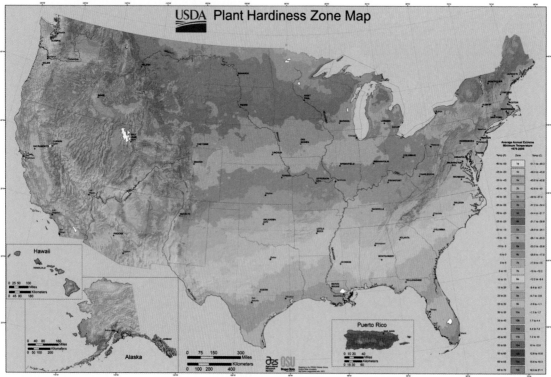

Credit: USDA Plant Hardiness Zone Map, 2012. Agricultural Research Service, U.S. Department of Agriculture. Accessed from https://planthardiness.ars.usda.gov/.

An easy first step is to check your hardiness zone. The USDA maintains the Plant Hardiness Zone Map (https://planthardiness.ars.usda.gov/), which can be used to help determine appropriate plants for your climate. It is divided into numbered 10-degree-Fahrenheit increments (further divided into two zones per number), based on average annual extreme minimum winter temperature (the lowest temperature it reaches on an average year). So for example, Minneapolis, Minnesota, is in Zone 4b, where the average annual extreme minimum temperature is -25 degrees, and about 30 miles north of there, you'll encounter Zone 4a, where the average minimum temperature is -30 degrees. For best results, select species that match your specific zone or are rated to a lower number. This will ensure that they are winter hardy in your area. Avoid plants that have a higher zone number than yours. They are more sensitive to cold temperatures and thus are unlikely to reliably survive over the long term.

SPACE CONSIDERATIONS

Whether you have a sprawling meadow or just enough space for a container garden (see page 264), the first step when planning a garden is to establish how much room is available, as the overall garden area directly influences plant selection. Avoid the temptation to overcrowd the available space. In other words, landscape for tomorrow, not today. Plants need room to grow, so think about how much space each plant will require once it matures, and be realistic. Use this guide and other resources to help determine each plant's height, overall form, and how much it spreads, and plan accordingly before putting it in the ground.

ANALYZE LIGHT LEVELS

The next step is to assess the specific characteristics of your site. It is important to evaluate the existing light, slope, moisture, drainage, elevation, and soil conditions. These environmental factors can significantly influence plant growth, performance, and even survival. Start with light level and slope exposure. Note how many hours of direct, unfiltered sunlight your proposed planting site receives in the summer. Plants labeled as **Full Sun** will thrive in sunny locations that receive at least 6 full hours of sunlight per day during the growing season. While such plants may still grow in locations that have less light, overall growth and flowering performance may be impacted, often severely.

Plants characterized as **Partial Sun** or **Partial Shade** typically perform best with 4–6 hours of direct sunlight a day or dappled light for the duration of the day. They often thrive when exposed to early day sun and may benefit from a bit less illumination during the hottest times of the afternoon.

Full Shade plants require less than 4 hours of direct sunlight. They often do quite well in locations with dappled shade and tend to prefer direct sun in the morning or the evening.

TAKING SLOPE AND ELEVATION INTO ACCOUNT

When you're evaluating your yard's light levels, keep slope exposure in mind, and note the direction a planting site is angled. An area's slope affects the amount of light it receives. North-facing slopes, for example, receive less direct sunlight. With reduced heating, they are cooler, and the soil tends to remain moist for a longer period of time. Such sites also experience a longer period of frost. By contrast, south- and west-facing slopes receive ample sunlight. They tend to be hotter

5

and have a somewhat longer growing season. With increased sun comes increased transpiration and evaporation, making such sites drier; this means they often require increased irrigation to maintain adequate soil moisture. Plants that are more heat and drought tolerant are often ideal for such exposures. While the impact of slope on your plantings can be subtle, it is nonetheless worth considering, especially at higher latitudes (30–55 degrees north), where slope can have a greater impact on light levels.

On a similar note, site elevation is also worth considering. High points in the landscape, such as along the ridge of a berm, are often more exposed to wind. This tends to dry out soil more rapidly, batters plants, and produces harsher winter conditions. Such locations are challenging for tender or delicate species, which prefer more-protected sites. Instead, choose drought-tolerant, more-robust plants.

ANALYZING MOISTURE LEVELS

Likewise, site moisture is vital to evaluate. Is the site in question consistently wet, moist, average, or dry? In most cases, you can tell simply by visually inspecting the site on a regular basis. Wet sites, for example, can be characterized as being reliably soggy, whereas moist sites are simply damp. Site location and drainage may also be useful. Is the site adjacent to a stream, wetland, or depression? Does rainwater regularly flow into or collect in the site? Soil composition and texture, such as the proportion of clay, silt, or sand present, directly impacts moisture retention and can be used to help assess site condition.

Testing soil texture

A SIMPLE SOIL TEXTURE TEST

If you're not sure, conduct a quick soil texture test. To do so, dig down about 6–8 inches with a shovel or trowel, and grab a handful of soil. First, rub a small amount through your fingers. How does it feel? Sandy soil is a bit coarse and feels somewhat gritty, whereas clay tends to feel a little sticky. Next, grab another handful. Moisten it slightly, squeeze into a ball, and then open your hand. Sandy soil tends to fall apart almost immediately. Loamy soil (which contains a mix of sand and clay) generally holds its shape but crumbles somewhat when prodded. Clay soil, by contrast, remains firmly together in a ball and resists breaking apart when pressure is applied.

SOIL TESTING

While it's not a necessity when planting a garden, it's often useful to get your soil tested. As soil properties directly affect plant growth and performance, knowing the pH level (how acidic or alkaline your soil is) and its nutrient levels can provide valuable insight, helping you select plants that are best suited for your specific conditions. Soil testing also helps you determine the best way to augment the existing soil and how to select the most efficient fertilizers if you opt to fertilize.

A pH test kit

Better yet, soil testing is simple and inexpensive. Most basic soil tests, which analyze pH, organic matter, and the levels of several basic essential nutrients are about $20 and often less. They're available at many home improvement stores, garden centers, and online. Local county extension offices also often test soil; for more information, including soil collecting procedures, laboratories available to analyze your sample, and costs, see page 274 for contact information.

When testing soil, be sure to test multiple areas, as soil conditions may vary depending on location and nearby trees/vegetation. If you really want to know everything about your soil, there are tests that go far beyond the basics, including tests for salt levels, trace elements, and even tests for lead contamination.

INTERPRETING SOIL TEST RESULTS

The chart below shows a number of common soil nutrients and micronutrients. When you get your soil tested, you'll receive a report indicating how acidic your soil is and the range of nutrients (and in some cases, micronutrients) present in your soil. You can then use this information when planning your garden and when preparing any future soil amendments.

Nutrient Levels and Micronutrient Ranges

pH 4.0	4.5	5.0	5.5	6.0	6.5	7.0	7.5	8.0	8.5	9.0	9.5	10.0

Acidic   Neutral   Alkaline

- Nitrogen
- Phosphorus
- Potassium
- Calcium
- Magnesium
- Sulfur
- Boron
- Copper
- Iron
- Manganese
- Molybdenum
- Zinc

Optimum Soil Availability

PLANNING AHEAD

In all cases, a little planning will produce better results: Your plants will perform better, your landscape will look more attractive, and most importantly, you (and the pollinators) will be happier. The cardinal rule is simple: pick the right plant for the location. For example, avoid forcing a sun-loving species into a shady spot. Instead, tailor your design and plant choices to your landscape's conditions. This is the only sure recipe for success.

WHEN TO PLANT

There is no hard-and-fast rule as to the best time to plant. Most gardeners are generally accustomed to planting in spring, once the growing season begins. This allows new plants ample time to get established, grow, and add beauty to your landscape. It also gives them a head start before the summer heat arrives, which can add to plant stress and necessitate more frequent irrigation. Planting during warm and dry conditions requires extra care and attention for best results, so keep this in mind if adding plants to your landscape during the summer months or during periods of abnormal heat or drought.

Fall planting is often ideal. The weather is often more predictable than in spring and the heat less intense compared to the peak of summer, especially in more northerly climates. The resulting more stable, mild conditions reduce plant stress. Soil temperatures are also quite warm, which helps stimulate root growth. Moreover, the germination of many weeds tends to wind down later in the season, which typically means less competition for the new plantings. Collectively, these conditions lead to increased plant growth and more rapid overall establishment. For best success, however, plan to get all plants in the ground with at least one month of the growing season remaining. This ensures that they have time to grow before increased chances of frost arrive. Fall is also an ideal time to divide perennials if needed.

Hand-removal works, but is labor intensive

ELIMINATING EXISTING WEEDS

Weeds are certainly one of the biggest challenges and frustrations in the garden. Unfortunately, there is no silver bullet for their control. Good site preparation prior to planting can make quite a difference, however. It can substantially minimize future weed pressure, and in turn, provides plants with better growing conditions. As with all other aspects of landscaping, it is useful to develop a detailed and realistic site-preparation plan and plan ahead before beginning.

In general, there are three main weed issues to consider. The first is obvious: eliminating existing weeds. Depending on the size of your site and the number of weeds, this can be done by simple hand-removal, or by weed torching, tilling, or applying a non-selective herbicide such as glyphosate directly to the weed foliage. If using a herbicide, be sure to carefully follow all the label instructions—to the letter—regarding application and safety. For larger sites, or sites with an increased weed load, herbicide application is typically the most labor- and cost-effective method. In this case, it is useful to mow the site, wait a few weeks until the weeds start to regrow, and then apply herbicide. A final mow (after a waiting period for the herbicide to take effect; see label) will then clear away most of the dead weed debris. In some cases, more than one cycle of herbicide application and mowing (spaced out about 2–4 weeks apart) may be necessary to get the best results. Note that for sites infested with weedy grasses, additional measures may need to be taken to produce effective control. When the weeds are removed, be sure to review the herbicide label for any potential residual effects that may negatively impact subsequent seeding or planting.

THE SEED BANK

The second weed-related issue to consider is the seed bank: weed seeds present in the soil that can germinate later, presenting a problem. If you want to avoid chemicals, soil solarization is one strategy to try. Popular in warmer southern climates, it's a bit trickier to attempt in the north, but it's worth attempting because of its many benefits. This simple method can be readily applied to both large or small areas. It involves covering existing soil with clear plastic and taking advantage of sunlight to heat the soil to a temperature that is sufficiently lethal to kill weeds, weed seeds, and potentially a range of soil pests and pathogens.

Soil solarization in progress

For best results, conduct soil solarization during the warmest months of the year. Start by clearing the area of all plants and associated debris. This ensures that the plastic can directly lay on the surface of the soil without large air pockets. Next, water the soil thoroughly. Moisture is a good conductor of heat and helps increase its penetration into the soil. Cover the area with clear plastic sheeting. Variously sized rolls of general purpose plastic sheeting can be purchased from home improvement stores or garden centers and are relatively inexpensive. It is useful to use a somewhat thicker (higher mil) product, usually 1.5 mil or greater, as it will help resist tears and punctures. Once the area is fully covered, bury the ends in soil or otherwise weigh them down with soil, bricks, lumber, or other material. This ensures that the plastic is sufficiently anchored and removes any air gaps, so that it can easily trap heat. To maximize effectiveness, it is generally recommended to leave the soil covered for 4 to 8 weeks.

Soil-applied herbicides are another option to combat the weed seed bank. These are applied to the soil after target plants have been established, and they create a barrier that kills weeds shortly after they germinate. They can provide effective residual control of various common broadleaf weeds and some annual weedy grasses for several weeks. Application may need to be repeated several times during the growing season for longer prevention. It is important to understand that no herbicide provides complete control and some products may injure existing plants or turf. As with other chemicals, always thoroughly read the label before use, and carefully follow the manufacturer's safety and application instructions.

NUISANCE WEEDS

The last main weed issue to address is nuisance weed control after plant establishment. Well-executed site preparation and planning can greatly reduce—but never completely eliminate—nuisance weeds. Beyond often being unattractive, weeds compete with your plants for resources, including light, water, and nutrients. Minor spot-weeding can often easily be done by hand or with the use of a weed torch. This should be done regularly for best control. Mulching is often one of the best ways to suppress nuisance weeds and significantly reduces the need for spot control, which can be time-consuming and inconvenient. Mulch also helps retain soil moisture and maintain a more consistent soil temperature, which can lessen plant stress, enhance plant growth, and reduce how much you need to water. Mulch can beautify an area by providing a more neat and manicured look. Many natural mulches even help add organic material to the soil over time as they decompose.

Compost is a popular soil amendment.

IMPROVING THE SOIL

Many soils require improvement to enhance their overall quality and structure. Organic matter such as compost, animal manure, straw, shredded wood chips, fallen leaves, and peat are common choices. These help improve fertility, water and nutrient retention, aeration, permeability, and other soil properties, which in turn promote healthy plant growth. Most organic amendments are easy to obtain. Compost, for example, is relatively simple to make or can be purchased from a local garden center. Be aware that some organic matter, such as animal manure, may contain weed seeds. Beyond organic matter, additional amendments such as sand, gravel, vermiculite, or perlite can also be used to help improve various soil properties. You can even use various amendments to tweak the soil pH or address key mineral or other nutrient deficiencies. Before doing so, consult your soil test results (see page 6), and use those results as a guide. You may also wish to get advice from a nursery professional or local extension agent.

NATIVE PLANTS MATTER

Studies have shown that including native plant species and increasing the overall plant diversity in your garden helps promote species diversity. Connecting these wildlife-friendly landscapes into a wider network—think of it as a pollinator trail of sorts—helps native pollinators and birds more easily and safely move from one place to another, maintains healthier wildlife populations and habitats, and improves or creates more opportunities for people to connect or reconnect with nature. By doing so, we can establish healthier and more-sustainable spaces for wildlife, and for humans.

PLANT LIFE CYCLE

Plants are generally characterized by their life cycle. While most woody plants are relatively long-lived, herbaceous species can be divided into three main categories: annuals, perennials, and biennials. Annuals complete their entire life cycle from initial germination to seeding in a single growing season. Only the seed, but not the plant, survives. Such species need to be planted anew each year or will germinate from seed dispersed by previous years' plants. Perennials, by contrast, survive and continue to grow for several years, with many surviving for much longer. Lastly, biennials take two years to complete development. The first year is one of leafy growth, while flowering and seed production are completed in the second full season. The original plant does not return for a third year of growth.

Black-eyed Susans

GARDEN DESIGN

Before you begin putting plants in the ground, it is helpful to make a basic plan or design sketch. Review the requirements and key features of each plant, such as light, moisture and soil preferences, mature size and spread, bloom time, flower color, leaf color, and fall color. Such information will help guide plant placement and your overall landscape design. Then, match plants with similar requirements together. Place the tallest plants in the back of the bed and shorter plants in the foreground, but keep light levels and sun direction in mind.

The total planting area available and its configuration will influence plant selection and quantity. For example, perennial boarders tend to be more narrow, linear spaces accessed from only one side. By comparison, cottage gardens can be more expansive and creatively designed. It is also often beneficial to group multiple plants of the same species together. Odd numbers of plant groupings are typically most visually pleasing, as this provides waves or blocks of color and texture in the landscape. For larval host plants, it also provides increased food resources for hungry larvae.

PLANT DIVERSITY

In general, increased plant diversity helps support a greater abundance and diversity of wildlife. If this is your goal, design your landscape accordingly. Pick plants that offer a wide range of quality resources of nectar, pollen, seed, fruit, and larval food. Be sure to include species that offer resources throughout the growing season, not just at one particular time period. This is particularly important for pollinating insects. Additionally, choose blooming plants that display a variety of flower color, size, and shape. For example, plants with long tubular blossoms may be most accessible and attractive to hummingbirds but not to smaller bees or butterflies. Lastly, pick plants that vary in height and form. This will provide needed structure in the landscape that in turn offers shelter, cover, nesting sites, perches, forage for food, or needed shade.

PLANT SELECTION AT THE NURSERY

Choosing plants for your landscape can be fun and highly rewarding. Nonetheless, some general best practices will help ensure the best possible outcome. Consult your yard inventory and remember to select plants that match the conditions of your property and the specific site in question. If you purchase plants from a home garden center, local nursery, or plant sale, take time to carefully inspect each one. When buying plants, be choosy. Examine all parts of the plant. Avoid plants with damaged stems, branches, or roots, yellowing or wilted leaves, or that otherwise have an overall unhealthy appearance. If you have doubts, it's probably good to stick with your instincts. Remember, you are making an investment in your property, so opt for the cream of the crop, such as plants with lush, robust, healthy foliage and a symmetrical form overall. These will likely perform best and make your landscape look its best.

Choose carefully when selecting plants.

When purchasing native plants or seed, especially through the mail, it is important to always select varieties that are native to your region and locality. This seed stock is adapted to the environmental conditions of your region, so the resulting plants will typically perform much better. For example, stock from North Carolina many not do as well in Minnesota or the rest of the Midwest, owing to differences in soil and climate. Purchasing local and regional ecotypes additionally helps safeguard the genetic integrity of native plants in your area.

CULTIVARS AND HYBRIDS

The topic of cultivars and hybrids is often highly contentious. Cultivars of native species, often referred to as "nativars," represent plants that have been specifically bred to select for a specific, desirable characteristic. This might include traits such as height, form, leaf color, or flower size or color. The resulting cultivars are often more flashy than their true native counterparts or offer additional options for gardeners that can add to their appeal and broad horticultural marketability. Commercial cultivars of many common natives, such as *Gaillardia, Liatris, Echinacea, Coreopsis,* and *Symphyotrichum* to name but a few, are readily available. Hybrids are reproductive crosses between two different but often closely related species with the goal of combining key features of both. Many cultivars are hybrids.

Be aware that there are potential drawbacks to some cultivars and hybrids, and many are often misleadingly sold as natives. Double- or triple-flowered varieties, for example, while attractive, often make it difficult for pollinators to access nectar and pollen. Many others are sterile and do not produce viable seeds or fruit. Others may lack nectar altogether or provide floral rewards with reduced nutritional benefits. These have limited value and attractiveness to landscapes designed to benefit birds, pollinators, and other wildlife. When in doubt, purchase plants from nurseries specializing in natives, or contact your local native plant society, botanical garden, arboretum, or extension office for recommendations on suppliers.

AVOID PLANTS TREATED WITH PESTICIDES

Avoid plants treated with pesticides.

Special care should be taken when purchasing plants that you hope will serve as larval hosts for caterpillars or as nectar plants for butterflies and other pollinating insects. Many plants sold at retailers, particularly those at larger garden centers, are often treated with pesticides to help control insect pests and resulting plant damage. While all pesticides pose a danger to insects, systemic pesticides, such as neonicotinoids, are among the most worrisome. Systemic pesticides are chemicals that are soluble in water and can be readily absorbed by a plant. They are relatively long-lasting to provide extended protection against sap- and leaf-feeding insects. Unfortunately, treated plants can be deadly to butterfly larvae, and there is evidence that some products contaminate flower pollen and nectar, resulting in potential harm to bees and other insect pollinators. Therefore, it is critical to always ascertain if the plants you're buying have been treated. Avoid treated plants, and if you're not sure about a plant, find a different supplier. Unfortunately there is no quick-and-easy test.

BEFORE YOU PLANT, STAGE YOUR GARDEN

When you're planning a garden, don't crowd plants. It's easy to forget that they will grow and increase in size, often dramatically, as they mature, so plan, and plant, accordingly. When your draft plan is finalized and you've acquired your plants/seeds, place all plants in their specific locations in the landscape and review. Look at the site from multiple angles, and adjust if needed. When happy, finish by putting all plants in the ground.

GIVING PLANTS A GOOD START

New plants perform their best with help right from the beginning. This includes initial planting. Start by digging a hole at least twice as wide as the root ball and just as deep. Next, gently remove the plant from its pot. Loosen the root ball by massaging the roots, separating them somewhat with your fingers, and place it in the hole. For bare-root plants, carefully spread out the roots when planting. Avoid placing the plant deeper than the original level in the pot, and do not place horticultural oil (a pesticide) on top of the root ball. Doing so can threaten the long-term health and performance of the plant. Once the root ball is in the hole, backfill with soil about half or three-quarters of the way upward, then gently tamp down the soil, and water. This will help the soil settle and remove any air pockets. Then fill the remainder of the hole with soil, and firmly compress it. Finally, water new plants regularly for at least the first three weeks. Following these steps will help ensure that your new plants have a strong start and are ready to perform.

MAINTENANCE

Most perennial plants, shrubs, and trees will thrive for years if well cared for. Do your homework to better understand the basic long-term needs of your plants, including watering, fertilization, pest and disease control, pruning, and winter care. Remember that a little basic planning and maintenance can make a huge difference. The goal is to have happy, healthy, and productive plants. A good example is pest control. While plant pests can be nuisance, all big issues start out small. By regularly examining your plants, you can easily discover pests before they become a larger problem. Once found, always address pest problems at a local level. Simply removing insect pests by pruning off the affected part of the plant or by spraying them with a strong jet of water can help significantly. Insecticidal soaps and horticultural oils can be good options, but they often can have negative impacts to the environment and non-target species.

Aphids and other insects may be annoying, but avoid broad-spectrum insecticides.

AVOID BROAD-SPECTRUM INSECTICIDES

Avoid or minimize the use of more-toxic broad-spectrum insecticides. These are designed to kill a wide range of insects and can harm many of the beneficial species that you wish to attract. If chemicals are used, always treat pest problems as locally as possible, and never spray or apply pesticides to the entire garden or landscape. Consult your local nursery professional or extension agent to help identify specific plant pest or disease issues and determine a viable solution. They can additionally help provide recommendations for effective pruning and fertilizing.

DEADHEADING

Many flowering perennials benefit from removing spent blossoms. Known as deadheading, this can help give plants a more manicured appearance and promote repeated blooming, which can in turn extend the flowering time of many species and provide added floral resources for pollinating insects. With that said, deadheading will prevent seeds or fruit from developing, and such food resources are also beneficial for many forms of wildlife, such as songbirds. So just how much to deadhead is something of a balancing act.

STAKING DOWN PLANTS

Some tall perennials or even newly planted trees may need to be staked. This can provide additional support and help prevent them from leaning, flopping over, or having weaker upright stems or flowering stalks bend or possibly break. Supports can also help elevate vines or rambling plants in the landscape, thereby enhancing their visual interest, appearance, and even performance

WHAT TO DO BEFORE WINTER

As winter approaches, there is often some debate about how to prepare your landscape—whether or not you should cut back the dead foliage on perennials or leave them standing. In general, this is more of an aesthetic issue than one of essential plant care. With landscapes designed for wildlife in mind, it is best to leave the dead foliage, stems, and flower heads in place. Not only do the remains of many flowering perennials and grasses provide highly attractive visual interest during the drab winter months, but various species also provide valuable food or shelter to songbirds and other wildlife. The exception is particularly tender perennials, such as those at the margin of their normal hardiness zone. Such plants often require a little extra care to help them survive frigid winter temperatures. Start by cutting off the dead vegetation just a few inches

Dead foliage helps out wildlife.

above the soil surface. Leaving a few inches of vegetation will help you keep track of the plant in your landscape and prevent any potential damage to the roots. Next, once the ground is frozen, cover the plant with several inches of mulch. This will help it conserve moisture and will insulate the soil, protecting it from extreme cold and the rapid freezing-and-thawing cycles that can result in soil heaving. Both can injure or even kill tender plants.

Spicebush Swallowtail butterfly on a Cardinal flower

The Basics of Plant Anatomy

Plants are complex living things. Their typical body plan consists of detailed structures, including leaves, stems, and roots, along with reproductive parts that include flowers, fruits, and seeds. Flowers represent the sexual reproductive organs of a plant. The male organs are called stamens; each stamen includes a pollen-bearing anther atop an elongated filament. The pistil represents the female organ. It

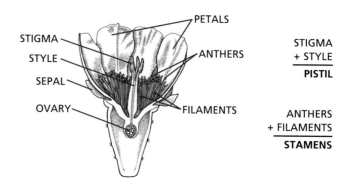

PARTS OF A FLOWER

includes a stigma, the surface of which is sticky. It receives and holds pollen. The majority of flowering plants that gardeners are familiar with are bisexual, or often called "perfect," and such plants have flowers with both male and female elements. Other plants bear unisexual flowers: Monoecious plants have both male and female flowers on the same plant. In contrast, dioecious plants bear male and female blooms on separate individual plants. Some examples of dioecious plants include holly (*Ilex* spp.), pussy willow (*Salix discolor*), and staghorn sumac (*Rhus typhina*).

FLOWERS

Flowers are arguably the showiest parts of a plant. In most cases, conspicuous and colorful petals surround the reproductive parts. They help publicize the availability of floral rewards, such as pollen and nectar, to an array of pollinating organisms. All the petals of a flower are collectively called the corolla. Sepals occur below the corolla. Like petals, they are modified leaves. Frequently green in color and relatively small, they help protect the developing flower bud and support the corolla when in bloom. This outermost whorl of flower components is called the calyx. In some cases, however, sepals may be large and brightly colored. This typically occurs in flowering plant species that lack petals.

FLOWER TERMINOLOGY

Botanically speaking, there are many types of flowers, but they can be simplified into five basic types. Regular flowers have a round shape with three or more petals and lack a disk-like center. Irregular flowers are not round, but uniquely shaped with fused petals. Bell flowers hang down with fused petals. Tube flowers are longer and narrower than bell flowers and point upwards. Composite flowers (technically a flower cluster) are usually compact round clusters of tiny flowers that look like they are one larger bloom.

Regular   **Irregular**   **Bell**   **Tube**   **Composite**

FLOWER CLUSTERS

The grouping of numerous flowers on a stem is called an inflorescence or a flower cluster. There are three main kinds of flower clusters, and they are based on shape: flat, round, or spike.

Flat   Round   Spike

LEAF TYPES

There are two main kinds of leaves: simple and compound. Simple leaves are leaves that are in one piece; the leaf is not divided into smaller leaflets. The leaf can have teeth or be smooth along the edges. It may have lobes and indentations that give the leaf its unique shape. Compound leaves have two or more distinct small leaves, called leaflets, arising from a single stalk. They can be broadly categorized as regular compound, twice compound, or palmate. Twice compound leaves are those with many distinct leaflets that arise from a secondary leafstalk. Palmate compound leaves have three or more leaflets arising from a common central point.

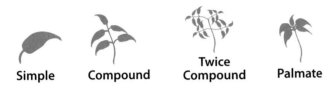

Simple   Compound   Twice Compound   Palmate

LEAF ATTACHMENTS

Leaves attach to the stem in a number of different ways: alternately, oppositely, in a whorl, perfoliately, clasping, or basally. Sometimes a plant can have two different types of attachment. This is most often seen in the combination of basal leaves and leaves that attach to the main stem. For most plants, there is only one type of leaf attachment.

Alternate leaves attach to the stem in an alternating pattern, while opposite leaves attach to the stem directly opposite from one another. Whorled leaves have three or more leaves that attach around the stem at the same point. Perfoliate leaves are stalkless and have a leaf base that completely surrounds the main stem. Clasping leaves have no stalk, and the base of the leaf only partially surrounds the main stem. Basal leaves originate at the base of the plant, near the ground, usually grouped in a rosette.

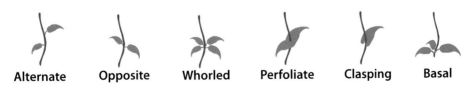

Alternate   Opposite   Whorled   Perfoliate   Clasping   Basal

Why Protect Pollinators?

Pollination is essential. Globally, over 80 percent of all flowering plant species rely on or benefit from animals, primarily insects, for pollination. These many organisms move pollen from one blossom to another, enabling the plants to produce fruit, seeds, and the next generation of flowering plants. Without pollinators, it would be impossible to maintain productive, diverse natural plant communities and ensure the functionality of our agricultural lands. Alarmingly, many recent studies indicate that insect pollinator populations are declining in many regions, including the United States and Europe. Some of the hardest-hit groups include bees, moths, and butterflies, important pollinators for many wild and cultivated plants, including various specialty crops. As habitat loss and degradation is a primary driver of these declines, rebuilding wildlife-friendly landscapes is more important than ever.

That's where you come in. Gardening for wildlife is a fun and rewarding endeavor. Now, more than ever, the choices we make in our own landscapes matter. While such spaces can never replace pristine natural environments, they can provide pollinators and birds with important food, nesting, and shelter resources and help reduce the many impacts of habitat fragmentation and urbanization. A growing body of research supports the wildlife conservation benefit of these non-traditional lands. Private yards and home gardens alone collectively comprise the largest percentage of green space in most urban areas. Additionally, as the majority of Americans now live in cities and their surrounding suburbs, yards and gardens offer tremendous potential for each of us to make a difference.

Meet the Pollinators

While bees, especially the western honey bee (*Apis mellifera*, also known as the European honey bee), get most of the attention, when it comes to pollination, many other insects regularly visit flowers and serve as pollinators. The most common groups include butterflies, moths, beetles, flies, and wasps.

BEES

North America boasts some 4,000 different bee species, with more than 500 species in the Midwest. With the exception of the non-native western honey bee and a few other introduced species, the rest are native, and the majority of bees actually lead solitary lifestyles. They also display a wide range of sizes, colors, and behaviors, making them fascinating and attractive garden visitors. Collectively, bees are arguably the most effective and efficient insect pollinators. Beyond visiting flowers for

nectar, they also actively collect pollen. These raw materials represent the primary food resources for adult bees and their developing young. In other words, they are highly motivated to make many flower visits and transport pollen, the components necessary for successful pollination. In addition, bees actively forage for floral resources in and around the landscape in which they nest. The majority of bees are generalists; like hungry patrons visiting a buffet, they visit a broad array of different flowers, preferring plants with large amounts of high-quality resources when available.

1. Western honey bee (*Apis mellifera*) **2.** Eastern bumblebee (*Bombus impatiens*) **3.** Eastern carpenter bee (*Xylocopa virginica*) **4.** Leaf-cutter bee (*Megachile* spp.) **5.** Sweat bee (*Agapostemon* spp., *Halictus* spp.) **6.** Long-horned bee (*Melissodes* spp.)

BUTTERFLIES

Butterflies are among the most recognizable and charismatic insects. Their tremendous appeal makes them ideal "gateway bugs" to help people connect with the natural world. Not surprisingly, butterfly gardening and butterfly watching are soaring in popularity nationwide. While the greatest diversity of butterflies occurs in tropical regions of the world, North America is home to around 800 different species, with around 200 species found in the Midwest.

All adult butterflies feed on liquids. Most species in our area consume sugar-rich nectar; this potent energy source helps power their flight and virtually all other activities. This is why butterflies are highly attracted to colorful blooming flowers. With the exception of the zebra longwing butterfly, which actively collects and feeds on pollen, all other species visit flowers to sip nectar. In the process of feeding, they often brush against the flowers' anthers and inadvertently pick up pollen on their head, body, or wings, making them important pollinators.

1. Tiger swallowtail (*Papilio glaucus*) **2.** Orange sulphur (*Colias eurytheme*) **3.** Gray hairstreak (*Strymon melinus*) **4.** Pearl crescent (*Phyciodes tharos*) **5.** Silver-spotted skipper (*Epargyreus clarus*) **6.** Peck's skipper (*Polites peckius*)

MOTHS

Compared to butterflies, moths are much more diverse. There are just 200 butterfly species in the Midwest, but there are perhaps nearly 1,400 species of moths, roughly 7 times as many. Despite this diversity, moths tend to be poorly studied and are often overlooked. As a result, relatively little is known about how much this primarily nocturnal group contributes to plant pollination. Nonetheless, recent research suggests that moths play a particularly important role as pollinators, including as pollinators of specialty agricultural crops, augmenting the work of bees and other flower-visiting insects. Moths may also help improve the genetic diversity of plants because they transport pollen over greater distances than bees. It is almost a certainty that additional studies will reveal that moths play a critical role as pollinators.

1. White-lined sphinx (*Hyles lineata*) **2.** Virginia ctenucha (*Ctenucha virginica*) **3.** Garden tiger moth (*Arctia caja*) **4.** Eight-spotted forester (*Alypia octomaculata*)

BEETLES

Beetles represent the largest and most diverse order of insects. In North American alone, there are approximately 28,000 species, and that's just a mere seven percent of the global total. Due to their tremendous numbers alone, beetles represent the largest group of pollinating animals, but not all beetles visit flowers. Those that do, visit in search of food, typically feeding on pollen, but they may also munch away on various flower parts and, less often, nectar. As beetles are typically somewhat clumsy, bulky insects, they need to physically land on and crawl across blossoms to feed, and in the process they frequently pick up pollen grains. They are most often encountered on larger open flowers or flowers with sizable clusters. This wonderful group of insects boasts a truly dizzying array of individual sizes, colors, and shapes, making observation fun and highly rewarding.

1. Goldenrod soldier beetle (*Chauliognathus pennsylvanicus*) **2.** Locust borer (*Megacyllene robiniae*) **3.** Hairy flower scarab (*Trichiotinus viridans*)

FLIES

With approximately 17,000 species found in North America, flies are another large and highly diverse group of insects, and a great many of them—even mosquitoes—frequent flowers. They typically feed on sugar-rich nectar, and occasionally pollen. Even though they have something of a negative reputation, flies are prolific and important pollinators, visiting a wide range of flowering plants, including many important crops, such as cherries, apples, pears, strawberries, and raspberries, among others. In addition, the larvae of many species play other key roles in the environment, including as predators that provide natural pest control or as decomposers, helping to break down dead plant or animal material. Some fly groups, such as hover flies (or flower flies), have a particularly strong predilection for flowers, and many species are highly convincing bee or wasp mimics.

1. Hover fly (Syrphidae family) **2.** Flesh fly (Sarcophagidae family) **3.** Green bottle fly (*Lucilia sericata*) **4.** Mosquito (Culicidae family) **5.** Crane fly (Tipulidae family)

WASPS

Together with bees and ants, wasps belong to the order Hymenoptera, the third-largest group of insects. Despite often being feared, the vast majority of wasps are actually solitary, nonaggressive, and don't pose a stinging hazard. By contrast, social wasps, such as yellow jackets, paper wasps, and hornets, can deliver a painful sting and will actively defend their nest if disturbed or threatened. Collectively, wasps are highly beneficial insects. Many are important pollinators that frequent a wide range of flowering plants. The adults are equally valuable predators or parasites of a wide range of insects, including many pest species. Taken as a whole, wasps are far more beneficial to the ecosystem—and to us—than we give them credit for.

1. Northern paper wasp (*Polistes fuscatu*) **2.** Bald-faced hornet (*Dolichovespula maculata*) **3.** Blue mud dauber (*Chalybion californicum*) **4.** Four-banded stink bug hunter wasp (*Bicyrtes quadrifasciatus*)

BEE MIMICS AND LOOKALIKES

Looks can be deceiving: a range of flower-visiting insects mimic bees or wasps, displaying superficially similar yellow-and-black color patterns to scare off would-be predators. While a great many of these lookalikes are flies, some day-flying moths and even a scarab beetle or two get in on the act. Thus, it is important not to jump to quick conclusions when you spot a brightly colored insect. It takes careful observation to recognize these superb disguises.

1. Syrphid fly (*Sphaerophoria philanthus*) **2.** Bee fly (Bombyliidae family) **3.** Thysbe hummingbird moth (*Hemaris thysbe*) **4.** Scarab (Scarabaeidae family) **5.** Wasp mimic moth (*Vitacea polistiformis*) **6.** Delta flower scarab (*Trigonopeltastes delta*)

BIRDS

Birds are popular and welcomed garden visitors. Beyond their broad appeal, birds provide a range of valuable services to the landscape. Ruby-throated hummingbirds are colorful and entertaining flower visitors that help pollinate numerous plant species. A great many birds, such as bluebirds, wrens, woodpeckers, swallows, and crows, also feed on insects. This is especially true during breeding season, when insects make up the majority of the high-protein diet adult birds feed to their young. In the process, they provide natural pest control and help keep plant-feeding insect populations in check. Still others help manage weeds by consuming large quantities of seed from aggressive or otherwise undesirable plants.

Fruit-feeding birds play a key role in seed dispersal. In fact, hundreds of plant species rely on our feathered friends for this valuable service. In doing so, birds help maintain healthy and diverse native plant populations.

Native Plant Conservation

Native plant populations are critical components of the ecosystem, so don't collect native plants or seeds from the wild. This can harm existing habitat, threaten local native plant populations, and adversely affect pollinators and other wildlife that rely on them for food. Additionally, in many instances, collecting native plants from the wild may be illegal. Instead, always purchase or acquire native plants from a reputable grower or source (see page 273 for recommendations).

How to Use This Book

All of the plants in this book are native plants, and they are organized by light requirements, with sections for Full Sun, Full Sun to Partial Shade, and Partial Shade to Full Shade. Each plant account includes information on the plant's size and growth pattern, hardiness zone, its bloom period, and what it attracts, as well as specific notes about the plant. When planning your garden, you can either find plants that strike your fancy by paging through the book, or you can consult the butterfly- and bee-specific garden plans on pages 260–263. If you're looking to attract a specific type of butterfly/ caterpillar, or hummingbirds, see page 270 for a list of larval hosts and page 269 for a list of plants that attract hummingbirds. And once you have your garden planned out, turn to page 273 for a list of some of the retail suppliers of native plants in the Midwest.

Midwest Plants at a Glance

With so many variables to consider, choosing plants for your garden can be a bit overwhelming. That's why we've created the following at-a-glance resource to help you decide what to plant.

It includes everything from hardiness zone, light level, and soil preference to blooming period and whether the plant attracts butterflies, bees, or birds.

Note: Browsing deer can cause damage to plants. While such feeding may simply be a nuisance, it can at times be quite destructive to a garden or landscape. Few plants are 100 percent deer-proof, especially if deer populations are large or available food resources are limited. Nonetheless, several species are considered moderately or highly resistant to deer, and they are indicated in the table that follows.

A wildflower garden in Minneapolis

	COMMON NAME	SCIENTIFIC NAME	LIGHT LEVEL	MIDWEST HARDINESS ZONE
	Anise Hyssop pg. 39	Agastache foeniculum	Full sun	5a–7b
	Big Bluestem pg. 41	Andropogon gerardii	Full sun	4a–7b
	Black-eyed Susan pg. 43	Rudbeckia hirta	Full sun	3a–7b
	Blue Flag Iris pg. 45	Iris virginica	Full sun	4a–7b
	Blue Vervain pg. 47	Verbena hastata	Full sun	3a–7b
	Butterfly Milkweed pg. 49	Asclepias tuberosa	Full sun	3a–7b
	Common Ironweed pg. 51	Vernonia fasciculata	Full sun	4a–7b
	Common Milkweed pg. 53	Asclepias syriaca	Full sun	3a–7b
	Common Ninebark pg. 55	Physocarpus opulifolius	Full sun	2a–7b
	Common Sneezeweed pg. 57	Helenium autumnale	Full sun	3a–7b
	Common Yarrow pg. 59	Achillea millefolium	Full sun	3a–7b
	Cross Vine pg. 61	Bignonia capreolata	Full sun	5b–7b
	Culver's Root pg. 63	Veronicastrum virginicum	Full sun	3a–7b
	Cup Plant pg. 65	Silphium perfoliatum	Full sun	4a–7b
	Downy Sunflower pg. 67	Helianthus mollis	Full sun	4a–7b
	False Aster pg. 69	Boltonia asteroides	Full sun	3a–7b
	Garden Phlox pg. 71	Phlox paniculata	Full sun	4a–7b
	Hoary Vervain pg. 73	Verbena stricta	Full sun	3a–7b
	Indian Blanket pg. 75	Gaillardia pulchella	Full sun	2a–7b
	Lanceleaf Coreopsis pg. 77	Coreopsis lanceolata	Full sun	3b–7b
	Large-flowered Beardstongue, pg. 79	Penstemon grandiflorus	Full sun	3a–7b

ATTRACTS BUTTERFLIES	ATTRACTS BEES	ATTRACTS BIRDS	SOIL PREFERENCE	BLOOMING PERIOD	DEER-RESISTANT
Yes	Yes	Yes	Dry	June–September	Yes
Yes	No	Yes	Average to dry	August–September	Yes
Yes	Yes	Yes	Average to dry	June–September	Yes
Yes	Yes	No	Average to wet	May–June	Yes
Yes	Yes	Yes	Moist to wet	July–September	Yes
Yes	Yes	Yes	Average to dry	June–August	Yes
Yes	Yes	Yes	Moist to wet	July–September	Yes
Yes	Yes	Yes	Average to dry	June–August	Yes
Yes	Yes	No	Average to dry	May–June	Yes
Yes	Yes	No	Moist to wet	August–October	Yes
Yes	Yes	No	Average to dry	June–September	Yes
No	Yes	Yes	Average	April–May	No
Yes	Yes	No	Moist	June–August	Yes
Yes	Yes	Yes	Average to moist	July–September	Yes
No	Yes	Yes	Average to dry	August–September	No
Yes	Yes	No	Average to moist	August–October	Yes
Yes	No	Yes	Average	July–September	No
Yes	Yes	Yes	Average to dry	July–September	Yes
Yes	Yes	No	Average to dry	June–September	Yes
Yes	Yes	Yes	Average to dry	May–August	Yes
Yes	Yes	Yes	Average to dry	May–June	Yes

	COMMON NAME	SCIENTIFIC NAME	LIGHT LEVEL	MIDWEST HARDINESS ZONE
	Leadplant pg. 81	*Amorpha canescens*	Full sun	2a–6b
	Little Bluestem pg. 83	*Schizachyrium scoparium*	Full sun	3a–7b
	Marsh Blazing Star pg. 85	*Liatris spicata*	Full sun	3a–7b
	Meadow Blazing Star pg. 87	*Liatris ligulistylis*	Full sun	3a–7b
	Meadowsweet pg. 89	*Spiraea alba*	Full sun	3a–7b
	New England Aster pg. 91	*Symphyotrichum novae–angliae*	Full sun	3a–7b
	Nodding Onion pg. 93	*Allium cernuum*	Full sun	3a–7b
	Ohio Buckeye pg. 95	*Aesculus glabra*	Full sun	3a–7b
	Orange Coneflower pg. 97	*Rudbeckia fulgida*	Full sun	3a–7b
	Pickerelweed pg. 99	*Pontederia cordata*	Full sun	3a–7b
	Prairie Dock pg. 101	*Silphium terebinthinaceum*	Full sun	4a–7b
	Purple Coneflower pg. 103	*Echinacea purpurea*	Full sun	3a–7b
	Purple Prairie Clover pg. 105	*Dalea purpurea*	Full sun	3a–7b
	Queen of the Prairie pg. 107	*Filipendula rubra*	Full sun	3a–7b
	Rattlesnake Master pg. 109	*Eryngium yuccifolium*	Full sun	3b–7b
	Rose Mock Vervain pg. 111	*Glandularia canadensis*	Full sun	5a–7b
	Roughleaf Dogwood pg. 113	*Cornus drummondii*	Full sun	5a–7b
	Showy Goldenrod pg. 115	*Solidago speciosa*	Full sun	3a–7b
	Showy Milkweed pg. 117	*Asclepias speciosa*	Full sun	3a–7b
	Showy Tick Trefoil pg. 119	*Desmodium canadense*	Full sun	3a–7b
	Sky Blue Aster pg. 121	*Symphyotrichum oolentangiense*	Full sun	3a–7b

ATTRACTS BUTTERFLIES	ATTRACTS BEES	ATTRACTS BIRDS	SOIL PREFERENCE	BLOOMING PERIOD	DEER-RESISTANT
Yes	Yes	No	Dry	June–July	Yes
Yes	Yes	Yes	Average to dry	August	Yes
Yes	Yes	Yes	Average to moist	July–September	No
Yes	Yes	Yes	Average to dry	August–September	No
Yes	Yes	No	Moist to wet	July–September	Yes
Yes	Yes	Yes	Average to moist	August–October	Yes
No	Yes	No	Average	June–August	Yes
No	Yes	Yes	Moist	April–May	Yes
Yes	Yes	Yes	Average to moist	June–September	Yes
Yes	Yes	No	Wet	June–September	No
Yes	Yes	Yes	Average	July–September	Yes
Yes	Yes	Yes	Average to dry	June–August	Yes
Yes	Yes	No	Average to dry	July–September	No
No	Yes	No	Moist to wet	June–August	Yes
Yes	Yes	Yes	Dry to moist	July–September	Yes
Yes	Yes	No	Average to dry	June–August	No
Yes	Yes	Yes	Moist	May–June	No
Yes	Yes	Yes	Average to dry	August–October	Yes
Yes	Yes	Yes	Average to dry	June–August	Yes
Yes	Yes	Yes	Average to moist	July–August	Yes
Yes	Yes	No	Average to dry	August–October	No

	COMMON NAME	SCIENTIFIC NAME	LIGHT LEVEL	MIDWEST HARDINESS ZONE
	Smooth Blue Aster pg. 123	*Symphyotrichum laeve*	Full sun	3b–7b
	Spotted Joe Pye Weed pg. 125	*Eutrochium maculatum*	Full sun	3a–7b
	Staghorn Sumac pg. 127	*Rhus typhina*	Full sun	3a–7b
	Stiff Goldenrod pg. 129	*Solidago rigida*	Full sun	3a–7b
	Swamp Rosemallow pg. 131	*Hibiscus moscheutos*	Full sun	5a–7b
	Trumpet Creeper pg. 133	*Campsis radicans*	Full sun	4a–7b
	Trumpet Honeysuckle pg. 135	*Lonicera sempervirens*	Full sun	4a–7b
	Virginia Mountain Mint, pg. 137	*Pycnanthemum virginianum*	Full sun	3b–7b
	Western Pearly Everlasting, pg. 139	*Anaphalis margaritacea*	Full sun	3a–7b
	Western Sunflower pg. 141	*Helianthus occidentalis*	Full sun	3a–7b
	White Prairie Clover pg. 143	*Dalea candida*	Full sun	3a–7b
	Wild Quinine pg. 145	*Parthenium integrifolium*	Full sun	4a–7b
	Winterberry pg. 147	*Ilex verticillata*	Full sun	5a–7b
	Yellow Coneflower pg. 149	*Ratibida pinnata*	Full sun	3a–7b
	American Basswood pg. 153	*Tilia americana*	Full sun to partial shade	3a–7b
	Black Cherry pg. 155	*Prunus serotina*	Full sun to partial shade	3a–7b
	Black Willow pg. 157	*Salix nigra*	Full sun to partial shade	4a–7b
	Blue Mistflower pg. 159	*Conoclinium coelestinum*	Full sun to partial shade	5b–7b
	Blue Wild Indigo pg. 161	*Baptisia australis*	Full sun to partial shade	3a–7b
	Bluebell Bellflower pg. 163	*Campanula rotundifolia*	Full sun to partial shade	3a–7b
	Brown-eyed Susan pg. 165	*Rudbeckia triloba*	Full sun to partial shade	3b–7b

ATTRACTS BUTTERFLIES	ATTRACTS BEES	ATTRACTS BIRDS	SOIL PREFERENCE	BLOOMING PERIOD	DEER-RESISTANT
Yes	Yes	No	Average to dry	August–October	Yes
Yes	Yes	No	Moist to wet	July–September	Yes
No	Yes	Yes	Average	June–July	No
Yes	Yes	No	Average	August–September	Yes
Yes	Yes	Yes	Moist to wet	July–September	No
No	Yes	Yes	Average	July–August	Yes
No	No	Yes	Average to moist	May–July	No
Yes	Yes	No	Average to moist	July–September	Yes
Yes	Yes	No	Average	July–September	Yes
No	Yes	Yes	Average to dry	July–September	Yes
Yes	Yes	No	Average to dry	June–August	No
No	Yes	No	Average to moist	June–September	Yes
Yes	Yes	Yes	Moist	June–July	No
Yes	Yes	No	Dry to moist	June–September	Yes
No	Yes	No	Average to moist	June	No
Yes	Yes	Yes	Average	April–May	No
Yes	Yes	No	Moist to wet	April–May	Yes
Yes	Yes	No	Moist	August–September	No
Yes	Yes	Yes	Dry to moist	May–July	Yes
Yes	Yes	No	Average to dry	June–September	Yes
Yes	Yes	Yes	Average to moist	July–September	Yes

Midwest Plants at a Glance (continued)

COMMON NAME	SCIENTIFIC NAME	LIGHT LEVEL	MIDWEST HARDINESS ZONE
Cardinal Flower pg. 167	*Lobelia cardinalis*	Full sun to partial shade	3a–7b
Common Boneset pg. 169	*Eupatorium perfoliatum*	Full sun to partial shade	3a–7b
Common Buttonbush pg. 171	*Cephalanthus occidentalis*	Full sun to partial shade	5a–7b
Common Hackberry pg. 173	*Celtis occidentalis*	Full sun to partial shade	2a–7b
Common Hoptree pg. 175	*Ptelea trifoliata*	Full sun to partial shade	3a–7b
Eastern Prickly Pear pg. 177	*Opuntia humifusa*	Full sun to partial shade	4a–7b
Eastern Redbud pg. 179	*Cercis canadensis*	Full sun to partial shade	4a–7b
False Indigo pg. 181	*Amorpha fruticosa*	Full sun to partial shade	4a–7b
Foxglove Penstemon pg. 183	*Penstemon digitalis*	Full sun to partial shade	3a–7b
Golden Alexanders pg. 185	*Zizia aurea*	Full sun to partial shade	3a–7b
Great Blue Lobelia pg. 187	*Lobelia siphilitica*	Full sun to partial shade	4a–7b
Halberd-leaf Rosemallow, pg. 189	*Hibiscus laevis*	Full sun to partial shade	4a–7b
Maryland Senna pg. 191	*Senna marilandica*	Full sun to partial shade	4a–7b
Michigan Lily pg. 193	*Lilium michiganense*	Full sun to partial shade	3a–7b
New Jersey Tea pg. 195	*Ceanothus americanus*	Full sun to partial shade	4a–7b
Northern Spicebush pg. 197	*Lindera benzoin*	Full sun to partial shade	4a–7b
Obedient Plant pg. 199	*Physostegia virginiana*	Full sun to partial shade	3a–7b
Ohio Spiderwort pg. 201	*Tradescantia ohiensis*	Full sun to partial shade	4a–7b
Partridge Pea pg. 203	*Chamaecrista fasciculata*	Full sun to partial shade	3a–7b
Pawpaw pg. 205	*Asimina triloba*	Full sun to partial shade	5a–7b
Pink Swamp Milkweed pg. 207	*Asclepias incarnata*	Full sun to partial shade	3a–7b

ATTRACTS BUTTERFLIES	ATTRACTS BEES	ATTRACTS BIRDS	SOIL PREFERENCE	BLOOMING PERIOD	DEER-RESISTANT
Yes	No	Yes	Moist	July–September	No
Yes	Yes	No	Moist to wet	July–September	Yes
Yes	Yes	Yes	Moist to wet	June–August	Yes
Yes	No	Yes	Moist	April–May	No
Yes	Yes	No	Average	May–June	Yes
No	Yes	No	Dry	June–July	Yes
Yes	Yes	Yes	Moist	April–May	Yes
Yes	Yes	No	Average to moist	June–August	Yes
Yes	Yes	Yes	Dry to moist	May–July	Yes
Yes	Yes	Yes	Average to moist	April–June	Yes
Yes	Yes	Yes	Moist to wet	July–September	No
Yes	Yes	Yes	Moist to wet	August–September	Yes
Yes	Yes	Yes	Average to moist	July–August	Yes
Yes	No	Yes	Moist to wet	June–August	No
Yes	Yes	Yes	Average to dry	June–August	No
Yes	Yes	No	Moist	March–April	No
Yes	Yes	Yes	Average to moist	July–September	Yes
No	Yes	No	Dry to moist	May–June	No
Yes	Yes	Yes	Average to dry	July–September	No
Yes	Yes	No	Moist	April–May	Yes
Yes	Yes	Yes	Moist to wet	July–September	Yes

	COMMON NAME	SCIENTIFIC NAME	LIGHT LEVEL	MIDWEST HARDINESS ZONE
	Purple Passionflower pg. 209	*Passiflora incarnata*	Full sun to partial shade	5a–7b
	Purplestem Angelica pg. 211	*Angelica atropurpurea*	Full sun to partial shade	4a–7b
	Pussy Willow pg. 213	*Salix discolor*	Full sun to partial shade	4a–7b
	Red Maple pg. 215	*Acer rubrum*	Full sun to partial shade	3a–7b
	Royal Catchfly pg. 217	*Silene regia*	Full sun to partial shade	4a–7b
	Sassafras pg. 219	*Sassafras albidum*	Full sun to partial shade	4a–7b
	Scarlet Bee Balm pg. 221	*Monarda didyma*	Full sun to partial shade	4a–7b
	Spotted Bee Balm pg. 223	*Monarda punctata*	Full sun to partial shade	3a–7b
	Tall Green Milkweed pg. 225	*Asclepias hirtella*	Full sun to partial shade	4b–7
	White Turtlehead pg. 227	*Chelone glabra*	Full sun to partial shade	3a–7b
	White Wild Indigo pg. 229	*Baptisia alba*	Full sun to partial shade	4b–7b
	Wild Bergamot pg. 231	*Monarda fistulosa*	Full sun to partial shade	3a–7b
	Wild Lupine pg. 233	*Lupinus perennis*	Full sun to partial shade	3a–7b
	Woolly Pipevine pg. 235	*Aristolochia tomentosa*	Full sun to partial shade	5a–7b
	Bigleaf Aster pg. 239	*Eurybia macrophylla*	Partial to full shade	3a–7b
	Common Blue Violet pg. 241	*Viola sororia*	Partial to full shade	3a–7b
	Cutleaf Coneflower pg. 243	*Rudbeckia laciniata*	Partial to full shade	3a–7b
	False Nettle pg. 245	*Boehmeria cylindrica*	Partial to full shade	3b–7b
	Purple Milkweed pg. 247	*Asclepias purpurascens*	Partial to full shade	4a–7b
	Red Columbine pg. 249	*Aquilegia canadensis*	Partial to full shade	3b–7b
	Sweet Joe Pye Weed pg. 251	*Eutrochium purpureum*	Partial to full shade	4a–7b

ATTRACTS BUTTERFLIES	ATTRACTS BEES	ATTRACTS BIRDS	SOIL PREFERENCE	BLOOMING PERIOD	DEER-RESISTANT
Yes	Yes	Yes	Average	May–June	Yes
Yes	Yes	No	Moist	May–June	Yes
Yes	Yes	No	Moist to wet	March–April	Yes
No	Yes	No	Moist	March–April	No
Yes	No	Yes	Average to dry	July–August	Yes
Yes	Yes	Yes	Average	April–May	Yes
Yes	Yes	Yes	Moist	July–September	Yes
Yes	Yes	Yes	Dry	July–September	Yes
Yes	Yes	Yes	Dry to moist	June–August	Yes
Yes	Yes	Yes	Moist to wet	July–September	Yes
No	Yes	No	Dry to moist	May–July	Yes
Yes	Yes	Yes	Dry to moist	July–September	Yes
Yes	Yes	No	Average to dry	May–June	No
Yes	No	No	Average to moist	May–July	Yes
Yes	Yes	No	Average to moist	August–October	No
Yes	Yes	No	Moist	April–June	Yes
Yes	Yes	Yes	Moist	July–September	Yes
Yes	Yes	No	Average to moist	June–August	No
Yes	Yes	Yes	Average to moist	June–July	Yes
Yes	Yes	Yes	Average to moist	April–June	Yes
Yes	Yes	No	Moist	July–September	Yes

	COMMON NAME	SCIENTIFIC NAME	LIGHT LEVEL	MIDWEST HARDINESS ZONE
	Virginia Bluebells pg. 253	*Mertensia virginica*	Partial to full shade	3a–7b
	Virginia Snakeroot pg. 255	*Aristolochia serpentaria*	Partial to full shade	5a–7b
	Wild Blue Phlox pg. 257	*Phlox divaricata*	Partial to full shade	3a–7b
	Woodland Sunflower pg. 259	*Helianthus divaricatus*	Partial to full shade	3a–7b

Winterberry, a native plant with bright red berries

ATTRACTS BUTTERFLIES	ATTRACTS BEES	ATTRACTS BIRDS	SOIL PREFERENCE	BLOOMING PERIOD	DEER-RESISTANT
Yes	Yes	Yes	Moist	April–May	Yes
Yes	No	No	Moist	May–June	Yes
Yes	Yes	No	Moist	April–June	Yes
Yes	Yes	Yes	Average to dry	July–September	No

Hoary Vervain

Indian Blanket

Full Sun

Rattlesnake Master

Cup Plant

Marsh Blazing Star

ig Bluestem

lack-eyed Susan

Common Ninebark

From black-eyed Susan (page 43) to large-flowered beardstongue (page 79), some of the plants we associate most with pollinators and hummingbirds thrive in full sun. These plants require at least six hours of direct sunlight, but that's the minimum. In many cases, they produce larger and more copious blooms if they have over 8 hours of sunlight, especially during the afternoon hours when the sun is at its strongest.

Common Ironweed

Prairie Dock

Anise Hyssop

Scientific Name *Agastache foeniculum*

Family Lamiaceae

Plant Characteristics Upright herbaceous perennial 2–4 feet in height; toothed leaves are somewhat elongated and heart-shaped; tubular lavender flowers grow as dense, slender terminal spikes on square green stems.

USDA Hardiness Zones 5a–7b

Bloom Period Summer–fall (June–September)

Growing Conditions Performs best in full sun and average-to-dry, well-drained soil.

This bushy perennial is a staple of many perennial, cottage, and herb gardens. Native to the northern tier of states, including the Upper Midwest, it boasts delightful licorice-scented foliage and a profusion of fuzzy, cylindrical flower heads that are virtually irresistible to pollinators. In fact, there is often a noticeable "buzzing" sound from the myriad of flower-visiting insects as one approaches the plant. Best grown in sunny locations with well-drained soil, anise hyssop is attractive individually or in a group. A vigorous grower under optimal conditions, plants form sizable clumps over time, are relatively drought tolerant, and freely self-seed. Several cultivars are commercially available. Its fragrant foliage also seems to deter deer and other mammals.

Extremely attractive to butterflies, bees, and other insect pollinators, as well as hummingbirds.

Big Bluestem

Scientific Name *Andropogon gerardii*

Family Poaceae

Plant Characteristics An upright perennial grass 4–8 feet in height; narrow leaf blades are bluish green to green; three-branched flowers are reddish purple.

USDA Hardiness Zones 4a–7b

Bloom Period Summer (August–September)

Growing Conditions Full sun and average-to-dry, well-drained soil.

Aptly named, big bluestem is a tall, clump-forming native grass of prairie habitats. Impressive in stature, mature plants typically dwarf those of little bluestem (page 83), a related species that is only two feet tall. Big bluestem adds both height and texture to larger landscapes. It is well suited for prairie gardens, wildflower meadows, or when clustered together for a prominent accent or as a backdrop for flowering perennials. Highly adaptable to most soil conditions, it is easy to grow, requires limited maintenance, and is quite drought tolerant once established. In late summer, the tops of plants are adorned with distinctive, three-branched flower heads that are said to resemble the shape of a wild turkey's foot. The foliage takes on a coppery red color as autumn progresses, with the rich tones lingering through the winter months. In more-ornamental spaces, gardeners may wish to cut the old growth back to the ground in spring. This provides a neater appearance and enables new foliage to emerge.

Serves as a larval host for the Arogos skipper (Atrytone arogos), *cobweb skipper* (Hesperia metea), *Delaware skipper* (Anatrytone logan), *and dusted skipper* (Atrytonopsis hianna).

Black-eyed Susan

Scientific Name *Rudbeckia hirta*

Family Asteraceae

Plant Characteristics Upright biennial or short-lived perennial (a perennial that only lasts a few years) 2–3 feet in height; leaves are coarse and green; daisy-like flowers are yellow with a dark-brown-to-black center atop stiff, slender stems.

USDA Hardiness Zones 3a–7b

Bloom Period Summer (June–September)

Growing Conditions Performs best in full sun and average-to-dry, well-drained soil, but it is highly adaptable to a wide range of soil types and conditions.

This cheerful and somewhat old-fashioned wildflower is a favorite in most Midwestern gardens. A fast grower and a highly resilient native, it can tolerate drought, heat, and poor soil. Black-eyed Susan is also easy to propagate by seed or division. Ideal for perennial borders, cottage gardens (small, informal, densely packed gardens), or for naturalizing, it produces a prolonged floral display and is a terrific pollinator attractor. Deadheading spent flowers will encourage reblooming. While generally short-lived as a perennial, the plants readily reseed and tend to pop up again year after year. Several commercial cultivars are available.

Highly attractive to butterflies, bees, and many other insect pollinators, it serves as a host plant for the gorgone checkerspot butterfly (Chlosyne gorgone).

Blue Flag Iris

Scientific Name *Iris virginica*

Family Iridaceae

Plant Characteristics Upright, herbaceous perennial 2–3 feet in height; green leaves are long, strap-like, and overlap at the base; flowers are broad and violet-blue. The large, downward-curving sepals have prominent yellow patches and noticeable dark veining.

USDA Hardiness Zones 4a–7b

Bloom Period Spring–summer (May–July)

Growing Conditions Performs best in full sun to partial shade and average-to-wet soil.

Also called Shreve's iris, this distinctive wildflower is a true wetland species. It is often encountered in marshes, damp woodlands, and along pond or stream margins. The shallow-rooted, leafy plants thrive in rich organic soil and can tolerate shallow standing water. While an obvious choice for rain gardens and water gardens, blue flag iris will perform well in more traditional perennial beds if the soil is kept consistently moist and never allowed to fully dry out. Individual plants expand into larger clumps over time and can spread by rhizomes, forming colonies. An early-season bloomer, the broad, arching flowers, each regularly measuring over three inches across, are visited by butterflies and larger bees.

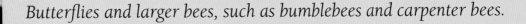

Butterflies and larger bees, such as bumblebees and carpenter bees.

Blue Vervain

Scientific Name *Verbena hastata*

Family Verbenaceae

Plant Characteristics Slender, upright herbaceous perennial 3–5 feet in height; long leaves are lance-shaped and serrated; tubular flowers are violet-blue and borne on dense, branched spikes atop stiff, somewhat reddish square stems.

USDA Hardiness Zones 3a–7b

Bloom Period Summer–fall (July–September)

Growing Conditions Performs best in full sun and fertile, moist-to-wet, well-drained soil.

This common wetland wildflower thrives in moist conditions. It is a great addition to wet meadows, pond or stream margins, rain gardens, or other habitually sunny but damp locations. It spreads readily by underground rhizomes and self-seeding, leading to the rapid formation of colonies. As a result, it can be a bit aggressive for smaller garden sites. Plants readily produce terminal arrangements of long, branched spikes that bloom from the bottom up. The individual tubular flowers, while small, have five flaring lobes and are quite showy. Collectively, the overall floral display is quite handsome and provides a bounty of resources for bees, butterflies, sphinx moths, and a wide range of other insect pollinators.

Highly attractive to butterflies, bees, and many other insect pollinators.

Butterfly Milkweed

Scientific Name *Asclepias tuberosa*

Family Apocynaceae

Plant Characteristics Distinctive upright herbaceous perennial 1–3 feet in height; leaves are narrow and oblong; flat clusters of flowers are light orange to deep-reddish orange. The plant forms dense, compact, multi-stemmed, and somewhat-arching clumps over time.

USDA Hardiness Zones 3a–7b

Bloom Period Summer (June–August)

Growing Conditions Full sun and average-to-dry, well-drained soil; it is drought tolerant once established.

Aptly named, this stunning native perennial is an absolute butterfly favorite. Its showy clusters of vivid orange flowers demand attention in any landscape and are highly enticing to a broad range of insect pollinators. It is arguably the most attractive and distinctive member of the milkweed genus (*Asclepias*). Perfect in sunny, dry locations, butterfly milkweed is a welcome addition to gardens of all sizes and styles, from smaller, more formal perennial borders to expansive wild prairie meadows. Elongated, spindle-shaped seedpods form after flowering and split open when mature to release numerous silky-tufted seeds that readily disperse by wind.

Very attractive to butterflies, bees, and other insect pollinators, as well as hummingbirds; a regular host plant for monarch caterpillars and those of the queen butterfly.

Common Ironweed

Scientific Name *Vernonia fasciculata*

Family Asteraceae

Plant Characteristics Stout upright herbaceous perennial 3–6 feet in height; leaves are narrow, lance-shaped, serrated, and dark green; dense, flat terminal clusters of flowers are light purple.

USDA Hardiness Zones 4a–7b

Bloom Period Summer–fall (July–September)

Growing Conditions Performs best in full sun and organically rich, moist-to-wet, well-drained soil.

Also called smooth ironweed or prairie ironweed, this is a widespread and relatively common species of marshes, roadsides, and open fields. While it prefers moist sites, common ironweed adapts well to fertile garden soil and is a great addition to rain gardens and wildlife gardens or the back of a perennial border. Plants readily self-seed and can spread aggressively, so some attention may be needed to curb colonization in smaller spaces. This same characteristic makes it a good choice for naturalizing in wetter prairies and meadows. The rich purple blooms pop against the traditionally abundant golden backdrop of the late-season landscape and are adored by butterflies and bees.

Butterflies, bees, and other insect pollinators.

Common Milkweed

Scientific Name *Asclepias syriaca*

Family Apocynaceae

Plant Characteristics Tall, upright herbaceous perennial 2–6 feet or more in height; green leaves are large and oblong; lavender flowers grow in showy rounded clusters. Common milkweed has a weedy growth habit; it spreads rapidly by rhizomes and can form extensive colonies.

USDA Hardiness Zones 3a–7b

Bloom Period Summer (June–August)

Growing Conditions Full sun and average-to-dry, well-drained soil; tolerant of poor soils and drought; easy to propagate from seed.

As its name implies, this native perennial is one of the most widespread and commonly encountered milkweeds in our region and a key larval host for the monarch butterfly. Regularly found along roadsides, fencerows, woodland borders, and in old fields and prairies, it is an aggressive colonizer of disturbed sites, spreading by both underground rhizomes and airborne seeds. Common milkweed is very easy to grow and fast to establish. The plant is tolerant of poor soil, drought, and neglect. Despite its weedy habit, it is a worthy addition to gardens and larger naturalized or wild spaces, as it adds unique texture and interest. A profuse bloomer, the large, rounded flower clusters perfume the air with a delightful fragrance and are exceptionally attractive to butterflies, sphinx moths, beetles, bees, and many other insect pollinators. Later in the season, the flowers give rise to large, elongated, and somewhat spiny seedpods that split open at maturity to release copious amounts of silky, tufted seeds that spread via the wind.

Very attractive to butterflies, bees, as well as hummingbirds. It is one of the most important hosts for monarch caterpillars.

Common Ninebark

Scientific Name *Physocarpus opulifolius*

Family Rosaceae

Plant Characteristics Deciduous shrub up to 8 feet in height; oval, lobed leaves are dark green; flowers grow in round terminal clusters of five-petaled white flowers.

USDA Hardiness Zones 2a–7b

Bloom Period Spring–summer (May–June)

Growing Conditions Full sun and average-to-dry, well-drained soil.

A fast-growing and exceptionally hardy native shrub, common ninebark is adaptable to a range of soil conditions and is tolerant of drought, once established. It has an attractive mounding growth habit with spreading branches and a distinctive exfoliating (peeling) bark. In early summer, plants produce dense rounded clusters of showy white flowers that provide abundant pollen and nectar for a broad range of pollinators. The flowers are followed by conspicuous pinkish brown seed capsules, which persist through the winter, providing interest to the late-season landscape. A wonderful addition to any garden, it can be grown as a hedge, an individual plant, or clustered together for year-round interest. This native plant remains somewhat underappreciated in terms of the benefit it provides to pollinators. Several commercial cultivars are available.

Butterflies, bees, flies, and other pollinators.

Common Sneezeweed

Scientific Name *Helenium autumnale*

Family Asteraceae

Plant Characteristics Upright, clump-forming herbaceous perennial 3–5 feet in height; lance-shaped leaves are serrated and dark green on distinctively winged stems; daisy-like flowers are golden yellow.

USDA Hardiness Zones 3a–7b

Bloom Period Summer–fall (August–October)

Growing Conditions Performs best in full sun and moist-to-wet, organically rich soil.

This plant's somewhat unfortunate name stems from a Menominee Indian practice of crushing dried leaves to produce sneezing. But in a garden setting, this flower is a delightful wetland perennial and won't provoke a trip to the medicine cabinet for allergy medication. A late-season bloomer, the toothed, wedge-shaped, bright-yellow petals surround a golden-bronze central domed cone, adding a profusion of autumnal color to the landscape. A wide variety of insect pollinators frequent the distinctive blooms. Common sneezeweed is a welcomed addition to rain gardens, pond margins, or larger wet meadows, as well as irrigated perennial borders. It is best planted en masse. Numerous ornamental cultivars are available.

Butterflies, bees, and many other insect pollinators. A larval host for Carmenta ithacae, *a type of clearwing moth, which get its name from its transparent wing segments.*

Common Yarrow

Scientific Name *Achillea millefolium*

Family Asteraceae

Plant Characteristics Upright to somewhat mat-forming perennial, 1–3 feet in height; ferny leaves are highly dissected and bright green; small white flowers grow in dense, flat-topped clusters atop upright leafy stems.

USDA Hardiness Zones 3a–7b

Bloom Period Summer (June–September)

Growing Conditions Performs best in full sun and average-to-dry, well-drained soil.

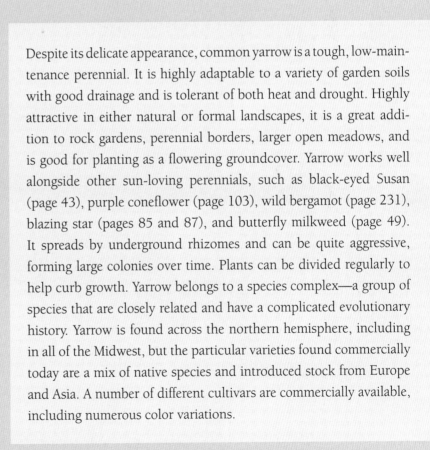

Despite its delicate appearance, common yarrow is a tough, low-maintenance perennial. It is highly adaptable to a variety of garden soils with good drainage and is tolerant of both heat and drought. Highly attractive in either natural or formal landscapes, it is a great addition to rock gardens, perennial borders, larger open meadows, and is good for planting as a flowering groundcover. Yarrow works well alongside other sun-loving perennials, such as black-eyed Susan (page 43), purple coneflower (page 103), wild bergamot (page 231), blazing star (pages 85 and 87), and butterfly milkweed (page 49). It spreads by underground rhizomes and can be quite aggressive, forming large colonies over time. Plants can be divided regularly to help curb growth. Yarrow belongs to a species complex—a group of species that are closely related and have a complicated evolutionary history. Yarrow is found across the northern hemisphere, including in all of the Midwest, but the particular varieties found commercially today are a mix of native species and introduced stock from Europe and Asia. A number of different cultivars are commercially available, including numerous color variations.

Highly attractive to butterflies, bees, wasps, and many other insect pollinators.

Cross Vine

Scientific Name *Bignonia capreolata*

Family Bignoniaceae

Plant Characteristics Woody perennial climbing vine to 35 feet or more in length; large leaves are dark green and compound, each with paired oblong leaflets; long, tubular flowers grow in axillary clusters and are pinkish orange with a yellow throat.

USDA Hardiness Zones 5b–7b

Bloom Period Spring (April–May)

Growing Conditions Performs best in full sun, average moisture, and well-drained soil.

Highly ornamental, this well-behaved woody vine is an excellent alternative to the more aggressive trumpet creeper (page 133). It is a high-climbing species that readily clings to structures via its branching, clawed tendrils; it works well when grown on a trellis, an arbor, a fence, a brick wall, or simply up a tree. The showy flowers vary somewhat in color and may be red on the outside with an orange or yellow throat. They are highly attractive to hummingbirds. Native to southern portions of the region, it often dies back to the ground and requires winter protection outside of its hardiness zone. Several commercial cultivars are available.

Hummingbirds, sphinx moths, and bees.

61

Culver's Root

Scientific Name *Veronicastrum virginicum*

Family Scrophulariaceae

Plant Characteristics Upright herbaceous perennial 4–6 feet in height; pointed leaves are whorled and scattered along sturdy green stems; small flowers are white to pale on dense, elongated terminal spikes.

USDA Hardiness Zones 3a–7b

Bloom Period Summer (June–August)

Growing Conditions Performs best in full sun and moist, well-drained fertile soil.

This striking native adds elements of elegance and verticality to the landscape. Each sturdy stem bears widely spaced whorled leaves that give the plant an airy appearance overall. Slender spikes of small, tubular flowers, many reaching six inches or more in length, begin to appear in early summer to midsummer. Additional smaller, branched lateral spikes result in a broad, eye-catching terminal arrangement that somewhat resembles a candelabra. Culver's root is a distinctive addition to sunny wetland edges, moist meadows, rain gardens, or the back of perennial borders. Plants are long-lasting under ideal conditions but are intolerant of prolonged drought. Plant them alongside Joe Pye weed (pages 125 and 251), pink swamp milkweed (page 207), blue vervain (page 47), cutleaf coneflower (page 243), and other moisture-loving bloomers.

Highly attractive to butterflies, bees, and many other insect pollinators.

Cup Plant

Scientific Name *Silphium perfoliatum*

Family Asteraceae

Plant Characteristics Stout upright herbaceous perennial 4–9 feet in height; large green leaves are opposite, clasping, and somewhat triangular with toothed margins; flowers grow as loose, branched terminal clusters and are bright yellow and sunflower-like on very tall, sturdy stalks.

USDA Hardiness Zones 4a–7b

Bloom Period Summer–fall (July–September)

Growing Conditions Performs best in full sun and organically rich, average-to-moist, well-drained soil.

This durable native is yet another truly unique and stately prairie plant. Cup plant is named for its large clasping leaves, which are fused to each other at their bases around the central stem. True to its name, the leaves form a basin that can actually hold rainwater. Plants expand into imposing multi-stemmed clusters that produce expansive terminal arrays of golden blooms in mid-to-late summer. The striking plants add texture and height to the landscape, soaring well over human height. The large, copious blooms are readily visited by butterflies, bees, and other flower-visiting insects. Plants spread vigorously by underground rhizomes and can rapidly expand into larger colonies. Like other members of the genus, this native plant is easy to cultivate and quite durable once established. Songbirds feed on the seeds and may occasionally sip water from the plant's natural "cups."

Butterflies, bees, and other insect pollinators.

Downy Sunflower

Scientific Name *Helianthus mollis*

Family Asteraceae

Plant Characteristics Upright herbaceous perennial 2–5 feet in height with large, downy, gray-green heart-shaped leaves and single golden yellow, daisy-like flowers supported on sturdy branched stems.

USDA Hardiness Zones 4a–7b

Bloom Period Summer–fall (August–September)

Growing Conditions Performs best in full sun and average-to-dry, well-drained soil.

Also called ashy sunflower, this wildflower is named for its characteristic foliage, which is covered in dense hairs, giving the plant a grayish appearance overall. Established plants give landscapes a wonderful combination of height, texture, and a distinctive color. Thriving in poor, average-to-dry soil, downy sunflower is easy to grow but can be quite aggressive, spreading rapidly by seed and rhizomes to form sizable dense colonies. As a result, it can often overwhelm small garden spaces and may best be used when naturalizing larger spaces. The bright, golden flowers are large and are especially attractive against the backdrop of its downy foliage. Once done blooming, the spent flower heads are popular with birds, which readily feed on the copious seeds.

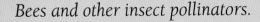

Bees and other insect pollinators.

False Aster

Scientific Name *Boltonia asteroides*

Family Asteraceae

Plant Characteristics Upright herbaceous perennial 3–5 feet in height; leaves are narrow and lance-shaped and become shorter up the plant; small daisy-like flowers are bright white with yellow centers and grow in terminal branched clusters.

USDA Hardiness Zones 3a–7b

Bloom Period Summer–fall (August–October)

Growing Conditions Performs best in full sun and average-to-moist, well-drained soil.

This handsome and underutilized perennial develops into sizable multi-stemmed clumps over time but is not aggressive in garden situations. While it thrives in organically rich, moist soil, false aster is highly adaptable to a variety of conditions, enduring both periodic drought and standing water. In late summer, plants begin to burst forth with a profuse array of small, brilliant white flowers. The resulting snowdrift-like effect is impressive, often earning this native the nickname of "thousand-flowered aster." A wide variety of pollinators—from butterflies and bees to wasps and beetles—take advantage of the abundant floral resources. False aster provides a showy pop of white to the late-season landscape, which is traditionally dominated by yellows and purples.

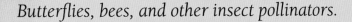

Butterflies, bees, and other insect pollinators.

Garden Phlox

Scientific Name *Phlox paniculata*

Family Polemoniaceae

Plant Characteristics Upright, unbranched herbaceous perennial 3–4 feet in height; green leaves are elliptical and pointed; tubular flowers are magenta, lavender, or white and grow in large terminal clusters.

USDA Hardiness Zones 4a–7b

Bloom Period Summer–fall (July–September)

Growing Conditions Performs best in full sun, average moisture, and organically rich, well-drained soil.

Also called summer phlox, this sturdy perennial is a familiar component of many perennial and cottage gardens. This sun-loving species thrives in fertile soil with average moisture and is intolerant of prolonged drought. Given the right conditions, though, plants expand to sizable, multi-stemmed clumps over time. Beginning in midsummer, the sturdy erect stems burst forth with impressive and abundant pyramid-shaped clusters of fragrant, five-lobed flowers that vary considerably in color. Cultivars are available in a variety of colors. Garden phlox makes an excellent cut flower, has a long blooming period, and quickly draws in hummingbirds and butterflies. Deadheading spent flower heads will promote reblooming.

Highly attractive to hummingbirds, butterflies, and sphinx moths.

Hoary Vervain

Scientific Name *Verbena stricta*

Family Verbenaceae

Plant Characteristics Upright clump-forming herbaceous perennial 2–4 feet in height; large gray-green leaves are oval-shaped with serrated edges; tubular purple-blue flowers grow in dense, slender terminal spikes atop sturdy stems.

USDA Hardiness Zones 3a–7b

Bloom Period Summer–fall (July–September)

Growing Conditions Performs best in full sun and average-to-dry, well-drained soil.

Although generally common and widespread in the wild, this handsome species is considerably underutilized in most landscapes. A short-lived perennial that may only survive for a year or so, it thrives in dry sites with poor soil. Despite its ephemeral nature, plants freely self-seed and thus can be a great choice for naturalizing an area. The sizable leaves are covered with fine hairs that give the plant an overall grayish green or "hoary" appearance. The flower spikes bloom from the bottom up. Five spreading lobes boast a long blooming period, often adding gorgeous purple flower spikes for up to six weeks in the late summer. After it's done flowering, this plant's seeds provide vital nourishment for a variety of small animals and birds, making it a perfect choice for any sustainable planting.

Highly attractive to butterflies, bees, and many other insect pollinators. Hoary vervain's leaves are also a common larval host for the common buckeye butterfly.

Indian Blanket

Scientific Name *Gaillardia pulchella*

Family Asteraceae

Plant Characteristics Compact annual 1–2 feet in height; hairy leaves are entire to toothed and mostly near the plant base; showy, daisy-like flowers have yellow-tipped red petals and contrasting purplish brown centers and grow atop slender branched stems.

USDA Hardiness Zones 2a–7b

Bloom Period Summer (June–September)

Growing Conditions Performs best in full sun and average-to-dry, often sandy, well-drained soil.

Also called firewheel, this striking wildflower adds intense, fiery color to the landscape. Its distinctive, showy blooms attract a bounty of insect pollinators. Songbirds may also feed on the seed from spent flower heads. Indian blanket is excellent for naturalizing in open meadows, prairies, and dry, disturbed sites. While most striking en masse, it can be used in smaller numbers or even planted individually in cottage gardens, rock gardens, flower borders, or even in container settings. Despite being an annual, it freely self-seeds and is easy to propagate by seed. Exceptionally easy to grow, it is tolerant of drought, heat, and poor soil but does not perform well in poorly drained sites. While thriving in dry, sandy soil, richer soil conditions tend to promote vegetative growth but poor flower production. Numerous commercial cultivars are also available.

Highly attractive to butterflies, bees, and many other insect pollinators.

Lanceleaf Coreopsis

Scientific Name *Coreopsis lanceolate*

Family Asteraceae

Plant Characteristics Compact herbaceous perennial 1–2 feet in height; hairy leaves are entire to deeply lobed; daisy-like flowers are bright golden yellow and grow atop erect green stems.

USDA Hardiness Zones 3b–7b

Bloom Period Spring–summer (May–August)

Growing Conditions Performs best in full sun and average-to-dry, well-drained soil.

This delightfully cheery perennial is a regular favorite of gardeners. A common addition to many wildflower seed mixes, it is an excellent choice for naturalizing in larger meadow or prairie landscapes. Plants freely self-seed and can quickly spread to form larger colonies. Plants started from seed will typically flower in their second year. Its compact growth habit makes it equally appealing for smaller gardens, perennial borders, or even container plantings. Exceptionally durable and easy to grow, lanceleaf coreopsis thrives in sunny, well-drained sites and is quite tolerant of heat, drought, and neglect once established. Plants produce profusions of showy yellow flowers that are beloved by a wide variety of insect pollinators; songbirds readily feed on the resulting seed. Deadheading spent flowers will promote reblooming and help prolong the floral display. Numerous ornamental cultivars are available commercially.

Butterflies, bees, and other insect pollinators. It is a larval host for the wavy-lined emerald moth and its highly camouflaged larva, which incorporates bits of plant tissue on its body as a disguise.

Large-flowered Beardstongue

Scientific Name *Penstemon grandifloras*

Family Scrophulariaceae

Plant Characteristics Upright herbaceous perennial 1–3 feet in height; large, rounded leaves are smooth and bluish green; large, tubular lavender flowers grow in loose terminal clusters.

USDA Hardiness Zones 3a–7b

Bloom Period Spring–summer (May–June)

Growing Conditions Performs best in full sun and average-to-dry, well-drained soil.

A wildflower of dry, poor soil, it is easy to grow in sites with good drainage and is very drought tolerant. Boasting showy blue-gray foliage that has a somewhat thick and smooth succulent-like feel, plants provide a distinctive look and texture to the landscape. The real appeal of large-flowered beardstongue, though, is obviously the species' conspicuous flowers, each up to an inch or more in length, with striped throats that guide foraging bees to the nectar. Hummingbirds are equally fond of the sizable blooms. It makes a unique early-season addition to rock gardens, perennial borders, or for naturalizing prairies or meadows.

Bees, sphinx moths, and hummingbirds.

Leadplant

Scientific Name *Amorpha canescens*

Family Fabaceae

Plant Characteristics Compact upright to spreading deciduous shrub 1–3 feet in height; compound leaves are delicate and gray-green; purple flowers grow in spikes and feature conspicuous bright-yellow anthers.

USDA Hardiness Zones 2a–6b

Bloom Period Early summer–midsummer (June–July)

Growing Conditions Best in full sun and dry, well-drained soil; it can tolerate a variety of soil types, including sand, gravel, and clay.

This lovely prairie shrub delights with showy, light-to-dark-lavender flower heads against a backdrop of fine, soft, and often silvery-looking foliage. Although easy to grow, it is often slow to establish and may take several years to flower. Over time, though, the plant develops a deep root system that renders it exceptionally durable and tolerant of drought, fire, and cold winter temperatures. Long-lived and distinctive, leadplant is an excellent choice for rock or native gardens, as well as for naturalizing larger meadows or prairie landscapes. Despite being woody, it often dies back to the ground each year before resprouting the following spring. A superb native for attracting wildlife, pollinators flock to the fuzzy blossoms. Unfortunately, they aren't alone; deer and rabbits also nibble on smaller plants.

Butterflies, bees, wasps, and other insect pollinators; southern dogface butterfly (Zerene cesonia) larvae consume the leaves, and songbirds enjoy the plentiful seeds.

Little Bluestem

Scientific Name *Schizachyrium scoparium*

Family Poaceae

Plant Characteristics Upright perennial grass 1.5–4 feet in height; spiky, narrow leaf blades are bluish green; purplish flowers (spikelets) are elongated and erect.

USDA Hardiness Zones 3a–7b

Bloom Period Summer (August)

Growing Conditions Full sun and average-to-dry, well-drained soil.

This upright, clump-forming grass is a dominant species of prairie systems. For landscape use, it offers outstanding year-round ornamental and wildlife value. As its name suggests, little bluestem has showy, finely textured bluish green foliage and a dense, mounding growth habit. It is ideal for naturalizing areas; when used grouped together en masse; or as an accent with flowering perennials. Later in summer, plants produce attractive but somewhat inconspicuous purplish flowers that are soon followed by fuzzy silvery seed heads that persist into early winter. The real show, however, starts in fall when the foliage transitions to a rich copper-burgundy color, providing wonderful visual interest during the dormant season. Easily grown and quite hardy, it accommodates a range of soil conditions but doesn't do well amid excessive moisture.

Beyond providing cover and food resources for a range of wildlife, it serves as a larval host for several butterflies, including the cobweb skipper (Hesperia metea), common wood nymph (Cercyonis pegala), crossline skipper (Polites origenes), dusted skipper (Atrytonopsis hianna), Indian skipper (Hesperia sassacus), Leonard's skipper (Hesperia leonardus), ottoe skipper (Hesperia ottoe), and the swarthy skipper (Nastra iherminier).

Marsh Blazing Star

Scientific Name *Liatris spicata*

Family Asteraceae

Plant Characteristics Upright herbaceous perennial 2–4 feet in height; basal leaves are long, dense, green and grass-like; small, tubular pink flowers are densely packed on tall, elongated spikes.

USDA Hardiness Zones 3a–7b

Bloom Period Summer–fall (July–September)

Growing Conditions Performs best in full sun and organically rich, average-to-moist, well-drained soil.

Arguably the most commercially available blazing star variety, this clump-forming perennial is a regular feature of many cottage gardens, perennial borders, and butterfly gardens. A plant of soggy meadows, prairies, and wetland margins, it thrives in sunny, moist sites but adapts well to home landscapes and can easily be grown in rich garden soil. It is also a superb species for naturalizing. Marsh blazing star boasts dense, mounding grass-like foliage that is perfect for creating soft texture in the landscape. Later in the summer, plants produce stout stems that terminate in elongated wand-like spikes, some well up to a foot or more in length. These spikes bloom from the top down, resulting in an explosion of pink flowers that are a favorite of butterflies, bees, and hummingbirds. Several cultivars are readily available that vary in color and form. The similar-looking meadow blazing star (page 87, *Liatris ligulistylus*) is slightly taller and prefers somewhat drier soil conditions. Both are wonderful in garden settings.

Butterflies, bees, and other insect pollinators.

Meadow Blazing Star

Scientific Name *Liatris ligulistylis*

Family Asteraceae

Plant Characteristics Upright herbaceous perennial 2–4 feet in height; basal leaves are green, long, dense, and grassy-like; flowers are light purple on elongated spikes of individual stalked heads.

USDA Hardiness Zones 3a–7b

Bloom Period Summer–fall (August–September)

Growing Conditions Performs best in full sun and average-to-dry, well-drained soil.

This distinctive wildflower is one of the most beautiful *Liatris* species. Also called Rocky Mountain blazing star, it is widespread across the western half of our region. Highly adaptable, it is easy to grow in most sunny garden locations that have well-drained soil. Once established, these durable plants are tolerant of drought and can readily handle the heat and humidity of summer. The showy flower stalks begin to appear in late summer. Each elongated inflorescence has a loose assortment of round, rosy stalked flower heads that appear to dot the stem. Monarchs are particularly fond of the blooms, as they provide reliable nectar resources during the start of the butterfly's annual mass fall migration. A wide assortment of other butterflies, bees, sphinx moths, and hummingbirds also visit the showy flowers. Best planted in numbers, meadow blazing star is perfect for naturalizing an area, or when clustered as an accent in butterfly gardens or perennial beds.

Butterflies, bees, and other insect pollinators, as well as hummingbirds.

Meadowsweet

Scientific Name *Spiraea alba*

Family Rosaceae

Plant Characteristics Upright deciduous shrub 3–6 feet in height; narrow lance-shaped leaves are sharply toothed and dark green; fuzzy white flowers grow in dense terminal clusters.

USDA Hardiness Zones 3a–7b

Bloom Period Summer–fall (July–September)

Growing Conditions Performs best in full sun and rich, moist-to-wet, well-drained soil.

This multi-stemmed shrub thrives in sunny, wet sites and is at home in moist prairies, damp meadows, or along streams or other wetland margins. While often best used in such landscapes, it can be grown in organically rich garden soil with regular irrigation. At first glance, the numerous slender green branches often resemble those of a perennial but become brown and woody with age. Meadowsweet spreads by suckering and can form small thickets over time. When used in smaller spaces, trim its suckers regularly to constrain expansion. Later in summer, the plant produces dense, elongated terminal clusters of white flowers that have long stamens and give the entire inflorescence (flower head) a noticeably fuzzy appearance.

Highly attractive to butterflies, bees, and other insect pollinators. It is used by the northern azure (Celastrina lucia) and spring azure (Celastrina ladon) butterflies as a larval host.

New England Aster

Scientific Name *Symphyotrichum novae-angliae*

Family Asteraceae

Plant Characteristics Stout upright herbaceous perennial 3–5 feet or more in height; narrow lance-shaped leaves are green to gray-green; daisy-like flowers are purple with yellow centers and grow in extensive terminal clusters.

USDA Hardiness Zones 3a–7b

Bloom Period Summer–fall (August–October)

Growing Conditions Performs best in full sun and organically rich, average-to-moist well-drained soil.

This stunning perennial is arguably one of our most beautiful native plants and a must-have for any pollinator garden. The sturdy reddish brown stems are encircled by hairy, distinctively clasping leaves. As autumn approaches, New England aster produces a profusion of magnificent blooms that range in color from deep purple to pink, highlighted by golden-yellow centers. While particularly showy en masse in prairie and meadow landscapes, individual plants or groupings add verticality and bright, rich hues to any cottage garden or perennial bed. For a particularly majestic effect, combine with goldenrods (pages 115 and 129), lanceleaf coreopsis (page 77), rudbeckias (pages 43, 165, and 243), or other yellow-flowered species. Beloved by pollinators, it represents a critical late-season resource for migrating monarchs and many other flower-visiting insects.

Butterflies, bees, and other insect pollinators; a larval host of the pearl crescent butterfly.

Nodding onion growing amid ferns

Nodding Onion

Scientific Name *Allium cernuum*

Family Amaryllidaceae

Plant Characteristics Small bulb 1–1.5 feet in height; leaves are narrow and grass-like; flowers grow in loose, nodding, rounded clusters and are light pink to lavender.

USDA Hardiness Zones 3a–7b

Bloom Period Summer (June–August)

Growing Conditions Performs best in full sun, average moisture, and well-drained soil.

Nodding onion is an easy-to-grow, low-maintenance native bulb. Its onion-scented grassy foliage and distinctive, pendulous blooms add beauty and soft texture to any landscape. Highly adaptable to a variety of soil conditions, from dry to moist, and drought tolerant once established, it is a superb addition to cottage gardens, perennial beds, or for naturalizing larger meadows. This charming species is especially showy when planted en masse. Plants readily self-seed or can be easily cultivated by transplanting small bulbs. The delicate pale blooms are highly appealing to bees.

Highly attractive to bees.

Ohio Buckeye

Scientific Name *Aesculus glabra*

Family Sapindaceae

Plant Characteristics Deciduous tree to 40 feet in height or more; leaves are large, palm-shaped, and compound, with 5–7 elliptical leaflets; tubular flowers are pale yellow and grow in upright terminal clusters.

USDA Hardiness Zones 3a–7b

Bloom Period Spring (April–May)

Growing Conditions Full sun to partial shade and moist, well-drained soil.

A distinctive native tree of moist habitats, it is commonly found in temperate hardwood woodlands and along rivers and streams. Ohio buckeye has an attractive, rounded growth habit, spreading branches, and large leaves, making it an ideal garden centerpiece or a shade tree. It is also a great addition to any woodland garden. In early spring, it produces showy, upright clusters of tubular flowers that are nearly a foot long and brighten the early season landscape. They are readily visited by ruby-throated hummingbirds and various native bee species. Its robust, rounded, spiky seed capsules develop later in summer. Each contains one or more shiny, dark-brown seeds with a characteristic light-brown spot or "eye," which is the origin of the species' common name. On a cautionary note, all parts of the plant are poisonous to humans and livestock if ingested.

Bees and hummingbirds.

Orange Coneflower

Scientific Name *Rudbeckia fulgida*

Family Asteraceae

Plant Characteristics Upright compact and mounding perennial 2–3 feet in height and just as wide; leaves are dark green; daisy-like flowers are yellow-orange with dark purplish brown centers atop stiff, slender stems.

USDA Hardiness Zones 3a–7b

Bloom Period Summer (June–September)

Growing Conditions Performs best in full sun and average-to-moist, well-drained soil; it is highly adaptable to a wide range of soil types and conditions, but it benefits from good air circulation.

An eye-catching and aptly named perennial, orange coneflower features brilliant yellow flowers that are tinged with orange. It is an easy-to-grow plant that rewards gardeners with a long blooming period, one that extends from midsummer well into fall. An excellent cut flower and extremely attractive to butterflies and other pollinators, this ornamental native also supports songbirds who feed on the late-season seed heads. Forming dense, mounding clumps, it is wonderful to plant either as individuals or en masse in cottage gardens, perennial borders, or other smaller landscapes. Combine orange coneflower with purple coneflower (page 103), blazing star (pages 85 and 87), or bee balm (pages 221 and 223) for an appealing display. Despite its compact growth habit, the species readily reseeds and additionally expands into small colonies through underground rhizomes. Orange coneflower is also pest- and deer-resistant.

Highly attractive to butterflies, bees, and many other insect pollinators.

Pickerelweed

Scientific Name *Pontederia cordata*

Family Pontederiaceae

Plant Characteristics Emergent aquatic or semi-aquatic perennial 1–3 feet in height; basal leaves are large, smooth, and heart-shaped; deep-violet-blue lobed flowers grow in an elongated dense spike borne on a stout sheathed stem.

USDA Hardiness Zones 3a–7b

Bloom Period Summer–fall (June–September)

Growing Conditions Performs best in full sun and shallow water to consistently waterlogged soil.

A true wetland plant, pickerelweed typically grows in shallow, still water. The large, shiny leaves arise from submerged rootstock and extend well above the waterline. But in a garden setting, it can tolerate soggy soil during drought conditions but should never be allowed to dry out. Plants spread by rhizomes and can readily form extensive colonies. The striking flower spikes draw in a wide assortment of butterflies, bees, and other insects and are particularly eye-catching en masse. While individual flowers are short-lived, larger colonies can produce blooms for an extended time. This unique plant is a colorful and distinctive addition to small water gardens, pond margins, or larger wetland landscapes.

Butterflies, bees, and other insect pollinators.

Prairie Dock

Scientific Name *Silphium terebinthinaceum*

Family Asteraceae

Plant Characteristics Upright herbaceous perennial 3–9 feet in height; huge green leaves are coarse and spade-shaped with toothed margins; sunflower-like flowers are golden yellow and grow in branching terminal clusters borne on very tall, sturdy stalks.

USDA Hardiness Zones 4a–7b

Bloom Period Summer–fall (July–September)

Growing Conditions Performs best in full sun, average moisture, and well-drained soil.

This is arguably one of the most distinctive and impressive prairie wildflowers. The plant boasts enormous basal leaves, many well over a foot long and about a foot wide. They are rough to the touch and have noticeably serrated edges. Collectively, they make a striking appearance in the landscape. Later in summer, plants shoot up robust flower stalks that tower above the surrounding vegetation and may reach up to 10 feet in height. They produce numerous showy yellow blooms that are readily visited by bees and other smaller pollinators. Because of its size, prairie dock is best used for naturalizing in more expansive prairie and wildlife landscapes or as a specimen in a larger perennial garden. Although plants are somewhat slow to establish and may take several years to flower, they are exceptionally tough and long-lived, often surviving for decades. When flowering is complete, many songbirds readily feed on the resulting seeds.

Bees and other insect pollinators.

Purple Coneflower

Scientific Name *Echinacea purpurea*

Family Asteraceae

Plant Characteristics Stout upright herbaceous perennial 2–5 feet in height; conspicuous, coarse green leaves get smaller up the stem; showy daisy-like flowers are pink to purple and occur singly atop stems.

USDA Hardiness Zones 3a–7b

Bloom Period Summer (June–August)

Growing Conditions Performs best in full sun and average-to-dry, well-drained soil. Although tolerant of poor soil and drought once established, richer garden soil and consistent moisture will enhance overall growth and flower production.

This popular native wildflower is easy to grow and an absolute must for any butterfly or pollinator garden. It is well suited for everything from small garden spaces to larger naturalized meadows or prairies. The showy and distinctive flowers begin to appear in midsummer and bloom profusely until early fall. The domed, spiny centers provide a sturdy landing platform for butterflies and other pollinators and easy access to abundant nectar. Purple coneflower is widely available commercially, and numerous striking cultivars exist in various colors. Regular deadheading of blooms will encourage continued flowering. Spent flower heads provide abundant seed resources for hungry songbirds, including goldfinches, cardinals, and others. Use in perennial beds with other sun-loving, shorter-lived perennials. Easily propagated by seed or root division. For a somewhat more delicate-looking alternative, try pale purple coneflower (*Echinacea pallida*), which grows well in similar conditions and freely self-seeds.

Highly attractive to hummingbirds, butterflies, bees, and many other insect pollinators.

Purple Prairie Clover

Scientific Name *Dalea purpurea*

Family Fabaceae

Plant Characteristics Upright, herbaceous perennial
1–3 feet in height; green leaves are finely dissected and
compound, each with numerous narrow oblong leaflets;
rosy-purple flowers grow in dense, compact cylindrical
spikes atop stiff green stems.

USDA Hardiness Zones 3a–7b

Bloom Period Summer–fall (July–September)

Growing Conditions Performs best in full sun and average-to-dry,
well-drained soil.

This graceful perennial is a favorite among pollinators. The showy,
thimble-shaped flower heads bloom from the bottom up, exploding
with a profusion of purple encircling a textured, grayish cone. Each
individual flower has yellow-orange anthers that collectively seem
to hover over the entire inflorescence like miniature satellites. As a
result, the dense flower heads are excellent sources of both pollen
and nectar. Individual plants produce numerous erect, unbranched
stems from the base that result in a somewhat rounded-to-spread-
ing bushy appearance. The fine, almost needle-like leaves add a soft
and airy texture to the landscape. Purple prairie clover is easy to
grow and highly adaptable to various soil conditions. Its plants are
also extremely durable, once established, making it a superb species
for naturalizing in dry prairies and meadows or plantings in smaller
perennial, rock, or cottage gardens.

*Butterflies, bees, and other insect pollinators; the southern dogface
butterfly (Zerene cesonia) uses it as a larval host.*

Queen of the Prairie

Scientific Name *Filipendula rubra*

Family Rosaceae

Plant Characteristics Tall upright herbaceous perennial 4–8 feet in height; palm-like leaves are deeply cut, serrated, and bright green; small pink flowers grow in dense, branched clusters atop sturdy stems.

USDA Hardiness Zones 3a–7b

Bloom Period Summer (June–August)

Growing Conditions Performs best in full sun and rich, moist-to-wet, well-drained soil.

Well-named, this stately and distinctive perennial is a stunner in the landscape. The large, fuzzy-looking branched clusters of light-pink flowers rise above much of the surrounding vegetation on tall, stout, and somewhat snaking stems. They bloom from the bottom up, and they offer no nectar, despite their showy appearance. Nonetheless, they provide ample pollen for bees and pollen-seeking insects. Even when not in flower, the bright, highly dissected leaves are quite ornamental. Queen of the prairie thrives in wet locations but adapts well to well-irrigated organically rich gardens. Queen of the prairie readily spreads by underground rhizomes to form colonies and is thus an excellent species for naturalizing larger landscapes. It is particularly eye-catching en masse but can overwhelm smaller garden spaces.

Highly attractive to bees.

Rattlesnake Master

Scientific Name *Eryngium yuccifolium*

Family Apiaceae

Plant Characteristics Upright herbaceous perennial 2–5 feet in height; leaves are narrow, elongated, and strap-like; small, rounded prickly heads of small white flowers are borne on tall, sturdy branched stalks. Overall the plant has a noticeably grayish green color.

USDA Hardiness Zones 3b–7b

Bloom Period Midsummer–early fall (July–September)

Growing Conditions Full sun and dry-to-moist, well-drained soil.

Without a doubt, this robust native is a distinctive addition to any open sunny landscape. Its stiff, grayish, primarily basal leaves resemble those of yucca and bear scattered teeth along the margin. In late summer, the plant sends up stout tall stalks that bear numerous, equally distinctive rounded (and quite bristly) flower heads. Although small and somewhat underwhelming in appearance, its flowers are regularly frequented by wide range of insect visitors, making it a must for any pollinator garden. Rattlesnake master makes an excellent accent when planted individually, and groups of plants are well-suited for perennial beds, cottage or wildlife gardens, or as part of a larger prairie planting or restoration. When planting, place rattlesnake master alongside other pollinator favorites, such as purple coneflower (page 103), blazing star (pages 85 and 87), butterfly milkweed (page 49), Culver's root (page 63), yellow coneflower (page 149), and purple prairie clover (page 105).

Particularly attractive to butterflies, sphinx moths, bees, and hummingbirds.

Rose Mock Vervain

Scientific Name *Glandularia canadensis*

Family Verbenaceae

Plant Characteristics Sprawling herbaceous perennial 0.5–1.5 feet in height; leaves are dark green, deeply lobed, and somewhat triangularly shaped; flowers are rose-pink to lavender and grow in broad, dome-shaped terminal clusters.

USDA Hardiness Zones 5a–7b

Bloom Period Summer (June–August)

Growing Conditions Performs best in full sun and average-to-dry, well-drained soil.

A handsome species, rose mock vervain has a somewhat mounding, creeping habit. It spreads by rooting stems along the ground and can form dense mats. It makes a colorful groundcover or a low-growing addition to rock gardens, perennial border edges, or other open, sunny locations. It's a tough plant that thrives in drier sites and grows well in poor soils, provided they are well-drained. The dark ferny foliage provides an attractive background for the prominent brightly colored verbena-like flower heads, which appear on ascending stems. Numerous pollinators, especially butterflies, sphinx moths, and bees, flock to the blooms.

Butterflies, bees, and other insect pollinators.

Roughleaf Dogwood

Scientific Name *Cornus drummondii*

Family Cornaceae

Plant Characteristics Large deciduous shrub to 20 feet in height; green leaves are large and oval; flowers are creamy yellow and grow in flat terminal clusters.

USDA Hardiness Zones 5a–7b

Bloom Period Spring–summer (May–June)

Growing Conditions Full sun and moist, well-drained soil.

This attractive native shrub is exceptional at attracting wildlife. Named for its upper leaf surfaces, which are rough to the touch, it is a fast-growing shrub that spreads readily by underground rhizomes, forming extensive colonies. A moisture-loving plant, roughleaf dogwood is ideal when naturalizing woodlands, wetland borders, or other moist sites. Its early-season flowers attract a bounty of pollinating insects, and they are replaced by showy white berries that are highlighted against the dark green leaves, which eventually turn a rich crimson in fall. The overall display is highly ornamental. Better yet, the fleshy fruit is a favorite of songbirds. The species is quite similar in appearance to the more widespread and abundant gray dogwood (*Cornus racemosa*), which tends to be shorter in stature and serves as a larval host for the summer azure butterfly (*Celastrina neglecta*).

Butterflies, the cecropia moth, bees, flies, and other pollinators.

Showy Goldenrod

Scientific Name *Solidago speciosa*

Family Asteraceae

Plant Characteristics Upright herbaceous perennial 2–5 feet in height; basal leaves are long, lance-shaped, and dark green; densely packed small yellow flowers grow on tall, elongated branching clusters borne on reddish stems.

USDA Hardiness Zones 3a–7b

Bloom Period Summer–fall (August–October)

Growing Conditions Performs best in full sun and average-to-dry, well-drained soil.

Perfectly named, showy goldenrod is arguably the most striking member of this diverse genus. It is an unbranched wildflower that expands into larger multi-stemmed clumps over time. Plants spread by underground rhizomes, making it ideal for naturalizing larger meadows or prairies. Note, however, that it can become a bit aggressive under ideal growing conditions. A durable perennial, it is tolerant of poor soil and dry conditions but thrives in regular garden soil, requiring little care and adding ornamental value to any perennial border, butterfly garden, or cottage garden. The elongated, plume-like flowers are distinctive and provide a wealth of resources for many foraging pollinators, doing so well into the fall.

Butterflies, bees, and other insect pollinators.

Showy Milkweed

Scientific Name *Asclepias speciosa*

Family Apocynaceae

Plant Characteristics Tall upright herbaceous perennial 2–4 feet in height or more; gray-green leaves are large and oblong; fragrant star-shaped flowers are light pink to rose-colored and grow in conspicuous round clusters.

USDA Hardiness Zones 3a–7b

Bloom Period Summer (June–August)

Growing Conditions Thrives in full sun and drier, well-drained soil but highly adaptable to a range of garden soils.

Appropriately named, this native is arguably one of our most handsome milkweeds. Found in western portions of the region, it is superficially similar to common milkweed (page 53) but has larger and more eye-catching blooms set against silvery-green leaves; it's also less aggressive when it comes to spreading. The two species occasionally hybridize. Easy to grow, very tolerant of poor soil, and drought tolerant once established, it is an excellent addition to any sunny wildlife garden or when used for naturalizing. Despite its many benefits, it remains a relative rarity in gardens.

Very attractive to butterflies, bees, and other insect pollinators, as well as hummingbirds; like other members of the genus, showy milkweed is a key monarch butterfly larval host; it's also a larval host for the queen butterfly.

Showy Tick Trefoil

Scientific Name *Desmodium canadense*

Family Fabaceae

Plant Characteristics Upright herbaceous perennial 3–5 feet in height; leaves are green and compound, each with three oval leaflets; large pea-like flowers are light pink to rose-colored and grow in elongated, dense terminal clusters.

USDA Hardiness Zones 3a–7b

Bloom Period Summer (July–August)

Growing Conditions Performs best in full sun and average-to-moist, well-drained soil.

Aptly named, this tall, somewhat sprawling wildflower is arguably one of the most attractive members of a notably weedy genus. It, like most other legumes, fixes atmospheric nitrogen into the soil, helping improve soil fertility. Plants are easily grown and very drought tolerant once established, and are best used in wildlife gardens, moist meadows, prairies, and other natural landscapes. Grouping plants together creates a conspicuous and appealing display. The handsome pink blooms are especially attractive to bees. After flowering, plants produce numerous flat, segmented seedpods. They are densely covered in fine hooked hairs that readily cling to passing organisms, helping the plants spread. Unfortunately, they also regularly adhere to clothing and can be a minor nuisance.

Bees and other insect pollinators; many game birds, such as turkey, quail, and pheasants, consume the seeds.

119

Sky Blue Aster

Scientific Name *Symphyotrichum oolentangiense*

Family Asteraceae

Plant Characteristics Upright herbaceous perennial 1–3 feet in height; elongated, oval green leaves become increasingly narrow up the stem; daisy-like flowers are light blue with bright-yellow centers and grow in loose terminally branched clusters.

USDA Hardiness Zones 3a–7b

Bloom Period Summer–fall (August–October)

Growing Conditions Performs best in full sun to partial shade and average-to-dry, well-drained soil.

A lovely wildflower of prairies, meadows, and thickets, sky blue aster offers a profusion of sky-blue flowers reminiscent of a cloudless late-summer sky. Like other asters, it is a late-season bloomer and a wonderful choice to add soft, airy color to the autumnal landscape. It is an easy species to grow, not overly particular about soil conditions, and quite drought tolerant once established. Plants spread by self-seeding and underground rhizomes, making it idea for naturalizing. It is particular showy alongside goldenrods (pages 115 and 129), sunflowers (pages 67, 141, and 259), and New England aster (page 91). The delicate flowers are broadly appealing to butterflies, bees, wasps, flies, and virtually any other insect pollinator.

Butterflies, bees, and other insect pollinators.

Smooth Blue Aster

Scientific Name *Symphyotrichum leave*

Family Asteraceae

Plant Characteristics Upright herbaceous perennial 2–4 feet in height; smooth, lanced-shaped, clasping leaves are bright green to somewhat gray-green; daisy-like flowers are pale lavender to blue with bright-yellow centers and grow in terminal branched clusters.

USDA Hardiness Zones 3b–7b

Bloom Period Summer–fall (August–October)

Growing Conditions Performs best in full sun and average-to-dry, well-drained soil.

This late-season wildflower is yet another enchanting aster worthy of adding to the landscape. It is named for its bright, clasping foliage that is noticeably smooth to the touch. Very easy to cultivate, smooth blue aster tolerates a wide range of soil and moisture conditions and does not readily spread. As fall approaches, plants produce an abundant array of pale-blue flowers that are a pollinator favorite. Great for mass planting in meadows or as a showy addition to any cottage or perennial garden. It is particularly showy combined with New England aster (page 91), purple coneflower (page 103), showy goldenrod (page 115), and Virginia mountain mint (page 137).

Butterflies, bees, and other insect pollinators. Serves as a larval host for the northern crescent butterfly (Phyciodes cocyta).

Spotted Joe Pye Weed

Scientific Name *Eutrochium maculatum*

Family Asteraceae

Plant Characteristics Upright herbaceous perennial 3–6 feet in height or more; highly textured, toothed green leaves occur in whorls that are spaced out along a stout purplish stem; fuzzy pinkish flowers grow in terminal, spreading, somewhat-flattened clusters.

USDA Hardiness Zones 3a–7b

Bloom Period Summer–fall (July–September)

Growing Conditions Performs best in full sun and moist-to-wet, fertile soil.

This is a widespread and statuesque wetland perennial. The plant's odd common name, Joe Pye, is reputed to stem from a somewhat-butchered transliteration of the name of an indigenous man who is purported to have used the plant as medicine in New England during the Colonial Period. Its stem is noticeably rosy and dotted with darker purple spots. At home in fens, marshes, and wet meadows or prairies, it is wonderful for naturalizing areas or in sunny, soggy, and often waterlogged landscape sites such as in rain gardens. It is particularly attractive when planted en masse. The multi-stemmed plants expand into sizable clumps with age and add an element of both height and texture. The large, fuzzy flower heads are a magnet for bees, butterflies, and other insect pollinators. It combines well with common boneset (page 169), blue vervain (page 47), and Culver's root (page 63).

Highly attractive to butterflies, bees, and many other insect pollinators.

125

Staghorn Sumac

Scientific Name *Rhus typhina*

Family Anacardiaceae

Plant Characteristics Upright deciduous shrub 10–25 feet in height; large compound leaves have numerous odd-numbered, lance-shaped toothed leaflets; small reddish yellow flowers grow in upright, cone-shaped clusters.

USDA Hardiness Zones 3a–7b

Bloom Period Summer (June–July)

Growing Conditions Full sun, average moisture, and well-drained soil.

This delightful native shrub is truly a plant for all seasons. Early in the year, it boasts shiny, green ferny foliage and upright, showy, pyramid-shaped flower clusters that draw in a multitude of smaller pollinators, from bees to beetles. As fall approaches, the flowers produce dense clusters of fuzzy, red berry-like fruit, and the leaves transition to yellow-orange and red in fall. The resulting display is a real showstopper, especially en masse. Birds readily covet the fruit, which often persists well into winter, providing yet more interest to the late-season landscape. Staghorn sumac spreads by suckering and quickly forms larger colonies. It is therefore ideal for naturalizing in open areas or along woodland margins. A vigorous grower, it is easily cultivated and adaptable to a range of conditions, but it's intolerant of wet, poorly drained sites.

Bees, flies, beetles, wasps; it's a larval host for the cecropia moth.

Stiff Goldenrod

Scientific Name *Solidago rigida*

Family Asteraceae

Plant Characteristics Upright herbaceous perennial 2–5 feet in height; large basal leaves are oblong and gray-green; densely packed small, yellow flowers grow in tall, flat-topped branching clusters borne on stout-leaved stems.

USDA Hardiness Zones 3a–7b

Bloom Period Summer–fall (August–September)

Growing Conditions Performs best in full sun, average moisture, and well-drained soil.

This native plant is a distinctive fall perennial that provides beauty and high-quality resources for pollinators. Stiff goldenrod is easy to cultivate and not overly particular about soil type or condition, provided it is well drained. The durable plants are quite tolerant of poor soil and drought. The species boasts characteristically large, floppy basal leaves that are covered in small white hairs, giving the vegetation an overall gray-green appearance. In later summer, plants send up tall, leafy stalks that support branched flat clusters of golden blooms, lasting well into fall. The bountiful resources are a magnet for monarchs and other insect pollinators. Goldenrods can be a bit weedy, spreading by both seed and underground rhizomes, and it may not be the best choice for smaller garden settings. It is, however, wonderful for naturalizing in meadows, prairies, or other open, sunny areas.

Butterflies, bees, and other insect pollinators.

Swamp Rosemallow

Scientific Name *Hibiscus moscheutos*

Family Malvaceae

Plant Characteristics Upright herbaceous perennial 4–7 feet in height; toothed leaves are broad and somewhat heart-shaped; large flowers are light pink to white with a crimson center.

USDA Hardiness Zones 5a–7b

Bloom Period Summer–fall (July–September)

Growing Conditions Performs best in full sun and moist-to-wet, fertile soil.

This stately wetland wildflower is at home in marshes, wet prairies, and along stream or pond margins. While thriving in wet, organically rich soil and even tolerating standing water, it is adaptable to more-traditional garden settings as long as there is regular irrigation and the soil is not allowed to dry out. Plants produce multiple sturdy stems and can form sizable shrubby clumps over time. It is a great addition to rain gardens, pond edges, or other perpetually soggy, sunny sites in the landscape. They are particularly impressive when planted in groups. The large dark-green leaves provide an excellent backdrop for the stunning flowers, which have five overlapping pale-pink-to-cream-white petals and a crimson center. This is also what gives the species another of its common names: crimson-eyed rose-mallow. Although short-lived, the enormous blooms can reach over six inches across and are abundantly produced on established plants. A wide array of pollinators flock to the open flowers.

Very attractive to butterflies, bees, and other insect pollinators, as well as hummingbirds.

Trumpet Creeper

Scientific Name *Campis radicans*

Family Bignoniaceae

Plant Characteristics Deciduous climbing vine to 35 feet or more in length; large leaves are dark green and compound, each with 7–11 elliptical toothed leaflets; long, tubular flowers are orange-red and grow in terminal clusters.

USDA Hardiness Zones 4a–7b

Bloom Period Summer (July–August)

Growing Conditions Performs best in full sun, average moisture, and well-drained soil.

A commonly sold native vine, trumpet creeper produces shiny green foliage and clusters of stunning tubular reddish flowers that are particularly attractive to hummingbirds. Plants are easy to grow and not particularly fussy, tolerating most garden soils. For maximum bloom production, plant them in sunny locations. Under favorable conditions, it is a vigorous grower and can be quite aggressive, using aerial rootlets to climb into trees or over other vegetation, much like ivy does. Plants also readily sucker from the ground. Use the species with caution in most smaller garden spaces, as it requires ample room and is best grown on structures and in isolation, well away from other plants that it may soon cover. Prune it to keep it under control. Several commercial cultivars are available, and they differ in flower color and growth habit.

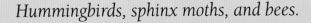

Hummingbirds, sphinx moths, and bees.

133

Trumpet Honeysuckle

Scientific Name *Lonicera sempervirens*

Family Caprifoliaceae

Plant Characteristics Deciduous twining vine up to 15 feet in length; smooth oval leaves are bluish green, with some often fused around the stem higher up on the plant; long tubular flowers are coral-red with a yellow interior and grow in loose clusters.

USDA Hardiness Zones 4a–7b

Bloom Period Spring–fall (May–July)

Growing Conditions Performs best in full sun and organically rich, average-to-moist, well-drained soil.

This delightful species is arguably one of our most attractive native vines. Its slender, twining habit is perfect for sunny fence-rows, arbors, and trellises. While it will tolerate some shade, flower production often dips or stops in shady areas. Plants boast both attractive shiny foliage and an abundance of flashy trumpet-shaped and somewhat pendulous blooms in late spring and early summer. The prominent coral-colored flowers have no fragrance but are an absolute magnet for ruby-throated hummingbirds. Once flowering is complete, the vine produces small, glossy red berries that are readily fed upon by songbirds.

Hummingbirds, sphinx moths, and some larger butterflies.

135

Virginia Mountain Mint

Scientific Name *Pycnanthemum virginianum*

Family Lamiaceae

Plant Characteristics Upright herbaceous perennial 2–3 feet in height; narrow, lance-shaped leaves are light green; small white flowers grow in flattened terminal clusters.

USDA Hardiness Zones 3b–7b

Bloom Period Summer–fall (July–September)

Growing Conditions Performs best in full sun and average-to-moist, well-drained soil.

This distinctive wildflower is an exceptional pollinator magnet. The multi-branched, compact plants have a bushy appearance overall and pleasing light-green fragrant foliage. Starting in midsummer and often continuing until early autumn, Virginia mountain mint produces dense terminal clusters of tiny white, purple-spotted tubular flowers. The copious blooms lure in a wide assortment of butterflies, bees, wasps, flies, and beetles. Better yet, Virginia mountain mint is very easy to grow and not overly fussy about soil type or condition. While it thrives in brightly lit, moist locations, it adapts quite well to garden soil and can even tolerate drought, once established. Plants expand to form small colonies over time, spreading readily by underground rhizomes. Because it's easy to grow, attractive, has a long blooming period, and attracts legions of pollinators, it's a top choice for pollinator and wildlife gardens or when used to naturalize larger landscapes.

Extremely attractive to butterflies, bees, and many other insect pollinators.

Western Pearly Everlasting

Scientific Name *Anaphalis margaritacea*

Family Asteraceae

Plant Characteristics Upright, clump-forming herbaceous perennial 1–3 feet in height; gray-green leaves are narrow and pointed; small yellowish flowers are surrounded by papery white bracts (modified leaves) and grow in flat-topped terminal clusters.

USDA Hardiness Zones 3a–7b

Bloom Period Summer–fall (July–September)

Growing Conditions Performs best in full sun to partial shade and average-to-dry, well-drained sandy or rocky soil.

A durable species of dry, poor soil in forest clearings, meadows, and waste areas, it is often found in larger colonies. The stems and leaves are densely covered in woolly white hairs, giving the plant a silvery appearance overall. While plants are somewhat raggedy-looking, the late season flowers are certainly worth the wait. Although they resemble petals, the showy papery white bracts completely surround and overshadow the plant's actual tiny yellow flowers. Numerous insect pollinators frequent the distinctive blooms. Aptly named, the terminal clusters of western pearly everlasting dry out and remain on the plant long after flowering is complete, making it an excellent addition to dried floral arrangements.

Butterflies, bees, and other insect pollinators. It is a larval host for the American lady butterfly (Vanessa virginiensis)*, which is also known as the American painted lady.*

Western Sunflower

Scientific Name *Helianthus occidentalis*

Family Asteraceae

Plant Characteristics Upright herbaceous perennial 1–4 feet in height; green basal leaves are large and oval; daisy-like flowers are golden yellow and grow in sparse branched clusters supported by tall leafless reddish stems.

USDA Hardiness Zones 3a–7b

Bloom Period Summer–fall (July–September)

Growing Conditions Performs best in full sun and average-to-dry, well-drained soil.

This somewhat compact species is a good sunflower for smaller landscapes. While plants spread via underground rhizomes and develop into larger clumps over time, they tend not to spread especially aggressively. Western sunflower additionally lacks the imposing stature that most gardeners come to expect with members of the sunflower family. In fact, these plants mostly have basal leaves that are easy to overlook amid a mix of surrounding vegetation. By mid-to-late summer, the real show begins. Tall, slender, and predominantly leafless reddish stems shoot skyward, supporting the showy blooms. The resulting effect, especially en masse, is quite distinctive and somehow graceful.

Bees and other insect pollinators.

White Prairie Clover

Scientific Name *Dalea candida*

Family Fabaceae

Plant Characteristics Upright, herbaceous perennial 1–2 feet in height; green leaves are finely divided and compound, each with numerous, narrow lance-shaped leaflets; small, white flowers grow in dense, compact cylindrical spikes atop stiff green stems.

USDA Hardiness Zones 3a–7b

Bloom Period Summer (June–August)

Growing Conditions Performs best in full sun and average-to-dry, well-drained soil.

A common prairie wildflower, this lovely perennial showcases pure-white, somewhat coarse-looking flower heads in summer. Each offers an abundance of nectar and pollen resources for insect pollinators, which frequent the dense spikes. Like purple prairie clover (page 105), white prairie clover's plants form multi-stemmed, somewhat bushy clumps but have noticeably larger leaflets. While easy to grow from seed, plants are generally slow to mature. But once they do, they thrive in drier conditions, aren't particularly fussy about specific soil composition, and are excellent for naturalizing larger areas. White prairie clover is very showy when combined with purple prairie clover (pager 105), butterfly milkweed (page 49), pale purple coneflower (page 103), black-eyed Susan (page 43), and other sun-loving perennials.

Butterflies, bees, and other insect pollinators. White prairie clover serves as a larval host for the southern dogface (Zerene cesonia) and Reakirt's blue (Echinargus isola) butterflies.

Wild Quinine

Scientific Name *Parthenium integrifolium*

Family Asteraceae

Plant Characteristics Upright herbaceous perennial 2–4 feet in height; large, green leaves are somewhat oval and coarsely toothed; small, white flower heads grow in several flattened terminal clusters supported on sturdy stems.

USDA Hardiness Zones 4a–7b

Bloom Period Summer–fall (June–September)

Growing Conditions Performs best in full sun and organically rich, average-to-moist, well-drained soil.

A somewhat distinctive clump-forming perennial of prairies and adjacent openings in dry woodlands and thickets, wild quinine prefers full sun and average soil moisture, but it can tolerate drought and some light shade. Also called American feverfew, the aromatic leaves and roots have several medicinal benefits and were used by Native Americans to treat burns, dysentery, and reduce fevers. The somewhat scaly-looking white flowers remain in bloom for an extended period and are regularly visited by wasps, flies, bees, small butterflies, and other pollinating insects. Often attractive en masse, wild quinine is best used when naturalizing a wilder garden space or in a perennial border. It is particularly showy when planted with more-colorful companions, such as purple coneflower (page 103), blazing star (pages 85 and 87), and black-eyed Susan (page 43).

Bees, wasps, small butterflies, beetles, moths.

Winterberry

Scientific Name *Ilex verticillata*

Family Aquifoliaceae

Plant Characteristics Deciduous shrub to 10 feet in height or more; green leaves are oval to elliptical; small white flowers grow in axillary clusters.

USDA Hardiness Zones 5a–7b

Bloom Period Summer (June–July)

Growing Conditions Full sun and rich, moist, well-drained soil.

Infrequently encountered in the wild, this deciduous native holly is a worthy landscape plant that is well suited when planting hedges, accents, or wildlife gardens. It has a dense, rounded growth habit and is easy to grow in moist, more-acidic soil. In early summer, plants produce an abundance of inconspicuous small white flowers. Despite their size, the blooms are frequented by bees and many other flower-visiting insects. Winterberry is dioecious, which means that some plants have male flowers, while others have female flowers. Fertilized flowers yield bright-red shiny berries. They persist on the plant well into the winter, giving this shrub its common name and adding needed color to the traditionally bare late-season landscape. Birds and other wildlife readily feed on the berries. Possumhaw (*Ilex decidua*) is a similar plant and a sound alternative, especially in southern portions of the region.

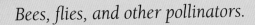

Bees, flies, and other pollinators.

Yellow Coneflower

Scientific Name *Ratibida pinnata*

Family Asteraceae

Plant Characteristics Graceful upright perennial 2–5 feet in height; green basal leaves are coarse and finely divided; large yellow flowers with drooping yellow petals sit atop tall, slender stems.

USDA Hardiness Zones 3a–7b

Bloom Period Summer (June–September)

Growing Conditions Performs best in full sun and dry or somewhat moist, well-drained soil; it is highly tolerant of a wide range of soil types and conditions.

This graceful wildflower is fast growing and a durable native. Easily propagated from seed, it is ideal for a variety of landscape uses, from naturalizing expansive areas to tucking it into the back of a sunny perennial border. Also called the gray-headed coneflower, the cone-like centers start out a gray-green color before turning a darker chocolate brown as they mature. Each flower has distinctive bright-yellow drooping petals that can often make the plant look a little raggedy. Yellow coneflower is a profuse bloomer and highly attractive to a wide range of insects, ranging from bees and flies to wasps and smaller butterflies. Yellow coneflower is excellent when combined with other sun-loving perennials, such as wild bergamot (page 231), butterfly milkweed (page 49), purple coneflower (page 103), scarlet bee balm (page 221), common milkweed (page 53), and blazing star (pages 85 and 87).

Highly attractive to butterflies, bees, and many other insect pollinators.

Foxglove Penstemon

Black Willow

Michigan Lily

Full Sun to Partial Shade

Eastern Redbud

Common Buttonbush

Bluebell Bellflower

Red Maple

From cardinal flower (page 167) to New Jersey tea (page 195), some pollinator- or wild-life-friendly favorites are somewhat adaptive when it comes to light level, performing well in either full sun or partial shade. These plants can tolerate 3–6 hours of direct sunlight per day but will often bloom more profusely with extended, but not direct, sunlight. Such plants are often good choices for open woodlands, forest margins, or other less-than-full-sun locations in the landscape.

Purple Passionflower

Eastern Prickly Pear

Cardinal Flower

American Basswood

Scientific Name *Tilia americana*

Family Malvaceae

Plant Characteristics Large deciduous tree to 80 feet in height; leaves are green and heart-shaped; small pale-yellow flowers grow in dangling clusters hanging from a leafy bract.

USDA Hardiness Zones 3a–7b

Bloom Period Summer (June)

Growing Conditions Full sun or partial shade and average-to-moist, well-drained soil.

A stately native, American basswood has a straight, pyramidal, and highly symmetrical growth habit with dense foliage, making it ideal as a shade tree or a centerpiece in home landscapes. In early summer, it produces an abundance of dangling flower clusters that are particularly fragrant and readily perfume the surrounding air. They are a favorite of honey bees, native bees, flies, and a range of other flower-visiting insects. Basswood is relatively fast growing and lives for up to a century. While it prefers moist conditions, it is somewhat tolerant of poor soil and drought once established.

Bees, flies, and other pollinators.

Black Cherry

Scientific Name *Prunus serotina*

Family Rosaceae

Plant Characteristics Deciduous tree to 80 feet in height or more; elliptical leaves are bright green; small white flowers grow in elongated pendulous clusters on young branches.

USDA Hardiness Zones 3a–7b

Bloom Period Spring (April–May)

Growing Conditions Full sun or partial shade, average moisture, and well-drained soil.

When it comes to attracting wildlife, this is an exceptional species, and it's also often overlooked for its ornamental value. It boasts appealing smooth, shiny green leaves and dark, flaky bark. In spring, black cherry produces a profusion of narrow, showy flower clusters, each up to six inches or longer. The copious blooms attract bees, flies, and other insect pollinators. The flowers are quickly replaced by clusters of small, round red fruits that mature to a purplish black color. They are a favorite food of many hungry songbirds. In fall, the green leaves turn a peachy-yellow to an orange-red, adding a wonderful pop of color to the landscape. Extremely fast growing and easy to cultivate, it can be somewhat weedy and aggressive, as it is readily spread by birds. Because of its many berries, it is messy and is not recommended near decks, driveways, or structures, as the dropping berries can leave stains. That said, it is great for naturalizing or even used as a centerpiece plant. For smaller landscapes, the similar-looking chokecherry (*Prunus virginiana*) is a good alternative.

Butterflies, bees, flies, and other pollinators. It serves as a larval host for the eastern tiger swallowtail (Papilio glaucus), red-spotted purple (Limenitis arthemis astyanax), and coral hairstreak (Strymon titus) butterflies.

Black Willow

Scientific Name *Salix nigra*

Family Salicaceae

Plant Characteristics Deciduous tree 80 feet in height or more; green leaves are long, narrow, and lance-shaped; cylindrical catkins are yellow to greenish and produced along the branches.

USDA Hardiness Zones 4a–7b

Bloom Period Spring (April–May)

Growing Conditions Full sun or partial shade and moist-to-wet soil.

This is a large, fast-growing tree that is commonly encountered in wetlands, seasonally flooded woodlands, and along streams and rivers. A moisture-loving species, it is tolerant of inundation but not of dry soil or drought. Trees may have single or multiple trunks and often have a spreading, somewhat irregular form. The species is dioecious, producing either male or female flowers on separate trees. The elongated catkins are produced in early spring as the leaves are emerging. They are visited for pollen and nectar by a tremendous assortment of pollinators. Pollinated flowers produce capsules that burst to release fuzzy, white cottony seeds.

Butterflies, bees, flies, and other pollinators; black willow serves as a larval host for the mourning cloak (Nymphalis antiopa), Acadian hairstreak (Satyrium acadica), and viceroy (Limenitis archippus) butterflies.

Blue Mistflower

Scientific Name *Conoclinium coelestinum*

Family Asteraceae

Plant Characteristics Compact branching herbaceous perennial 1–3 feet in height; leaves are bright green and prominently veined; flowers are fuzzy and light blue and grow in flat-topped clusters atop upright purplish green stalks.

USDA Hardiness Zones 5b–7b

Bloom Period Summer–fall (August–September)

Growing Conditions Performs best in full sun to partial shade and rich, moist soil.

This distinctive wildflower is also called hardy ageratum due to its resemblance to the common garden annual. It thrives in perpetually moist locations but is adaptable to garden settings as long as the soil is rich with organic material and it's regularly irrigated. Established plants can tolerate some drought, especially in partially shaded areas, but they perform poorly without consistent moisture. A somewhat weedy plant for small spaces, blue mistflower spreads aggressively via underground rhizomes or seed, often forming dense stands. This growth habit makes it an excellent choice for naturalizing in wetland gardens, open woodlands, or along streams or ponds. A late-season bloomer, its plants produce a profusion of dense powdery-blue flower clusters that are highly enticing to a wide range of insect pollinators.

Butterflies, bees, and other insect pollinators.

Blue Wild Indigo

Scientific Name *Baptisia australis*

Family Fabaceae

Plant Characteristics Robust upright herbaceous perennial 2–4 feet in height and just as wide; foliage is green to somewhat bluish green; pea-like flowers are light to dark blue and grow in elongated spikes. Blue wild indigo forms expanding, multi-stemmed shrubby clumps over time.

USDA Hardiness Zones 3a–7b

Bloom Period Late spring to summer (May–July)

Growing Conditions Full sun to partial light shade and a variety of dry or somewhat-moist, well-drained soils.

This bushy native is one of the most widely cultivated members of the genus *Baptisia* and a true garden favorite. Although somewhat slow to establish, the plant expands into sizable and dense, multi-stemmed clumps over time. Highly attractive individually or when planted in smaller groups, it is easy to grow, durable, and can be incorporated into more-formal perennial borders as well as wild, natural spaces. A dwarf variety is also available for smaller landscapes. The stately plants produce numerous long, upright spires of striking blue flowers that are readily visited by bumblebees. Later in the season, the vibrant flowers give way to inflated, dull-black seed pods for continued interest and appeal.

*Particularly attractive to bumblebees, but butterflies and hummingbirds occasionally visit the blooms. The species is periodically used by the wild indigo duskywing (*Erynnis baptisiae*) as a larval host plant.*

Bluebell Bellflower

Scientific Name *Campanula rotundifolia*

Family Campanulaceae

Plant Characteristics Upright herbaceous perennial 0.5–1.5 feet in height; basal leaves are small, dark green, and heart-shaped, and slender stems bear linear grass-like leaves; violet flowers are showy and bell-shaped and grow individually or in loose clusters.

USDA Hardiness Zones 3a–7b

Bloom Period Summer–fall (June–September)

Growing Conditions Performs best in full sun to partial shade and average-to-dry, well-drained soil.

Also called harebell, this graceful perennial adds a colorful splendor to the landscape. Starting in late spring, the plant bursts forth with characteristic nodding bell-shaped flowers that are supported on graceful, thread-like stalks. The striking violet blooms may continue to be sporadically produced throughout the summer, especially if they are regularly deadheaded. They are primarily visited by bees but also by some butterflies. Despite their delicate appearance, the compact plants regularly thrive in harsh soil conditions and are quite drought tolerant. Bluebell bellflower is an ideal choice for cottage or rock gardens, smaller perennial beds, or for naturalizing in open woodlands, rocky slopes, or meadows. Grouping several plants together provides the best visual impact.

Butterflies and bees.

Brown-eyed Susan

Scientific Name *Rudbeckia triloba*

Family Asteraceae

Plant Characteristics Upright biennial or short-lived herbaceous perennial 2–3 feet in height; coarse green leaves are entire to lobed; daisy-like flowers are yellow with a dark brown to black center and sit atop stiff, reddish brown branched stems.

USDA Hardiness Zones 3b–7b

Bloom Period Summer–fall (July–September)

Growing Conditions Performs best in full sun to partial shade and average-to-moist, well-drained, fertile soil.

While this attractive wildflower thrives in organically rich, moist locations, it is highly adaptable to a variety of garden conditions and relatively tolerant of heat, drought, and poorer soil. Established plants produce bushy, densely branched clumps that yield an impressive profusion of golden-yellow blooms, each with conspicuously dark centers. The resulting display can be quite spectacular and provides an abundance of resources to bees, butterflies, and a wide assortment of other insect pollinators from midsummer until the first hard frost. Regular deadheading of spent flowers promotes reblooming. Although short-lived, plants freely self-seed, even becoming a bit weedy. Showy en masse or individually, brown-eyed Susan is a welcomed addition to any perennial border, meadow, or wildlife garden, and when planted along moist woodlands or wetland margins.

Highly attractive to butterflies, bees, and many other insect pollinators.

Cardinal Flower

Scientific Name *Lobelia cardinalis*

Family Campanulaceae

Plant Characteristics Herbaceous perennial 2–5 feet in height; lance-shaped leaves are dark green; lobed tubular flowers are bright red and grow in spikes borne on sturdy upright stalks.

USDA Hardiness Zones 3a–7b

Bloom Period Summer–fall (July–September)

Growing Conditions Performs best in full sun to partial shade and rich, moist soil.

This stunning species is named for its vibrant cardinal-red tubular blossoms that are a favorite of ruby-throated hummingbirds. Some larger butterflies, such as swallowtails, also frequent the blossoms. A moisture-loving perennial, it is a showy addition to regularly soggy sites, rain or wetland gardens, or pond and stream borders. It is adaptable to more-traditional perennial garden settings with fertile, highly organic soil as long as regular irrigation is provided. It is intolerant of drought, and sites where it is planted should not be allowed to dry out. Plants are short-lived and typically persist for only a few years, but they freely self-seed as well as reproduce via basal offshoots. The resulting seedlings and young plants grow quickly. Winter mulching is beneficial to help provide insulation from temperature extremes. Cardinal flower is generally deer resistant.

Hummingbirds and butterflies.

Common Boneset

Scientific Name *Eupatorium perfoliatum*

Family Asteraceae

Plant Characteristics Upright herbaceous perennial 3–5 feet in height or more; highly textured green leaves are compound, and their bases merge together around the central stem; fuzzy white flowers grow in terminal, somewhat flattened clusters.

USDA Hardiness Zones 3a–7b

Bloom Period Summer–fall (July–September)

Growing Conditions Performs best in full sun to partial shade and moist-to-wet, fertile soil.

As the "common" in its name implies, this is a widespread and commonly encountered wetland wildflower. It is a distinctive plant, with long and arching bright-green and copiously veined leaves that fuse together around a noticeably hairy stem. Later in summer, plants produce handsome branched clusters of small, white flowers that give the entire flower head a somewhat fuzzy appearance. Common boneset thrives in perpetually moist, organically rich soil and is a wonderful addition to a stream or pond margin, a soggy woodland border, an open wetland, or a rain garden. Plants spread by underground rhizomes to form larger colonies over time. It is highly attractive when combined with marsh blazing star (page 85), blue vervain (page 47), spotted Joe Pye weed (page 125), cutleaf coneflower (page 243), and other moisture-loving perennials.

Highly attractive to butterflies, bees, and many other insect pollinators.

Common Buttonbush

Scientific Name *Cephalanthus occidentalis*

Family Rubiaceae

Plant Characteristics Deciduous shrub 6–12 feet or more in height; leaves are bright, shiny, green, and elliptical; dense, spherical clusters of tiny, white tubular flowers are produced on long stalks along the stems.

USDA Hardiness Zones 5a–7b

Bloom Period Summer (June–August)

Growing Conditions Performs best in full sun to partial shade and moist-to-wet soil.

A distinctive shrub of wetland habitats, common buttonbush thrives in consistently moist conditions and can withstand periodic inundation. Despite this preference, it adapts well to most organically rich garden soils that have regular irrigation. Plants have a lovely arching form and are generally spread much wider than their overall height. They showcase attractive, glossy green foliage and truly unique, round flower clusters, each about the size of a ping pong ball. Every tiny flower displays a single white style that projects well beyond the petals and gives the overall cluster a characteristic pincushion-like appearance. The fragrant blooms are exceptionally attractive to pollinators, drawing in a wide assortment of butterflies, bees, wasps, flies, and even an occasional hummingbird. Numerous birds feed on the resulting seed. This species is outstandingly wildlife-friendly and a great addition to a rain garden, pollinator garden, pond or stream margin, or for naturalizing in wetter areas of the landscape. Several cultivars are available with more compact growth habits. **Note:** This plant is toxic if ingested.

Butterflies, bees, and other insect pollinators, as well as hummingbirds.

Common Hackberry

Scientific Name *Celtis occidentalis*

Family Cannabaceae

Plant Characteristics Deciduous tree to 60 feet in height; green broadly lance-shaped leaves have serrated margins; small, yellow-green flowers lack petals.

USDA Hardiness Zones 2a–7b

Bloom Period Spring (April–May)

Growing Conditions Full sun or partial shade and rich, moist, well-drained soil.

An abundant and widespread native tree, common hackberry features grayish bark, a broad crown, and wide, arching branches, making it a great landscape choice. It is also a useful addition to any moist woodland site or for use along waterways. A relatively fast grower, it is tolerant of a range of conditions, including poorer soil and increased shade. The early spring flowers are small and easily overlooked, but they soon develop into fleshy purple-black berries that attract a range of songbirds, including cedar waxwings, robins, cardinals, and northern mockingbirds, even well into early winter.

Butterflies; hackberry serves as a larval host for several butterflies, including the American snout (Libytheana carinenta), *the hackberry emperor* (Asterocampa celtis), *the tawny emperor* (Asterocampa clyton), *the question mark* (Polygonia interrogationis), *and the mourning cloak* (Nymphalis antiopa).

Common Hoptree

Scientific Name *Ptelea trifoliata*

Family Rutaceae

Plant Characteristics Deciduous tree up to 20 feet in height; leaves are bright green, shiny, and compound, with each having three elliptical leaflets; greenish white flowers grow in terminal clusters.

USDA Hardiness Zones 3a–7b

Bloom Period Spring–summer (May–June)

Growing Conditions Full sun or partial shade, average moisture, and well-drained soil.

This small but handsome tree often features several ascending branches from the base, making it appear more like a shrub. This ornamental growth habit combined with a rounded crown make it a perfect accent plant for smaller landscapes. The airy flower clusters appear in spring among the leaves, attracting a wide assortment of insects. After flowering, trees produce dangling clusters of distinctive, round, wafer-like winged fruit, which helps give the species its other common name of wafer ash. (The fruits also bear a passing resemblance to hops, explaining its other name.) The shiny leaves have a strong citrus odor when crushed.

Butterflies, bees, flies, and other pollinators; it is a larval host plant for the giant swallowtail (Papilio cresphontes).

Eastern Prickly Pear

Scientific Name *Opuntia humifusa*

Family Cactaceae

Plant Characteristics Upright to sprawling, clump-forming cactus 0.5–2 feet in height; oval green pads are fleshy and flattened and have numerous small tufts of fine sharp bristles; flowers are large and waxy-looking.

USDA Hardiness Zones 4a–7b

Bloom Period Summer (June–July)

Growing Conditions Performs best in full sun to partial shade and thin, dry, well-drained sandy or rocky soil.

While cacti may seem oddly out of place in Midwestern gardens, this delightful species is widespread throughout southern portions of our region but highly underutilized in the landscape. A clump-forming plant, eastern prickly pear is a distinctive and highly ornamental addition to sunny, dry garden locations. It thrives in sandy or rocky sites but is somewhat tolerant of other soil types provided they are well-drained. The fleshy, evergreen pads have scattered darker bumps called areoles, which bear numerous small barbed hairs and often a longer sharp spine. Be careful when handling or working near these well-defended plants. The dramatic bright-yellow flowers, often measuring more than three inches across, start appearing in early summer along the upper pad margins. They are particularly appealing to bees, beetles, and other insects seeking nectar and copious amounts of pollen. Over time, the blooms are replaced by equally appealing barrel-shaped, reddish brown fruits that also bear sharp hairs. Prickly pears are easy to propagate: simply remove one of the pads and place the cut end in soil.

Bees, beetles, flies, and other insect pollinators.

Eastern Redbud

Scientific Name *Cercis canadensis*

Family Fabaceae

Plant Characteristics Small deciduous tree to 30 feet in height; large green leaves are heart-shaped; small pea-like flowers are rose-pink and grow in clusters on short stalks along the branches.

USDA Hardiness Zones 4a–7b

Bloom Period Spring (April–May)

Growing Conditions Full sun or partial shade and moist, well-drained soil.

Eastern redbud is a distinctive and highly ornamental native. Prior to the leaves emerging, its bare branches explode with profuse clusters of rich, rosy-pink flowers that brighten up the early-season landscape. It makes a wonderful specimen, grouped together or combined with white-flowering dogwoods for a real pop of spring color. The spring blooms attract a multitude of insect pollinators, from butterflies to bees and many more. The single trunk often branches close to the ground, adding interest and supporting a graceful, spreading but often irregular crown packed with large, heart-shaped leaves. Easily grown and long-lived, it benefits from consistent moisture, but soil must be well drained. Several commercial cultivars are available.

Butterflies, bees, flies, and other pollinators; serves as a larval host for Henry's elfin butterfly (Callophrys henrici).

False Indigo

Scientific Name *Amorpha fruticosa*

Family Fabaceae

Plant Characteristics Tall, upright, and multi-stemmed deciduous shrub 6–15 feet tall; leaves are green and compound; spikes of purple flowers bear conspicuous bright-yellow anthers.

USDA Hardiness Zones 4a–7b

Bloom Period Summer (June–August)

Growing Conditions Full sun or partial shade and average-to-moist, well-drained soil; it is highly adaptable to a variety of different garden soil types and conditions.

This fast-growing shrub has a loose, airy growth habit, with much of its foliage appearing on the upper half of the plant. The lower stems are woody and generally bare, giving it somewhat of a scraggly appearance. Plants can spread quickly by seed and root suckers. Despite its preference for consistent moisture, false indigo is quite tolerant of poor soil and dry conditions. It can also be periodically pruned to improve overall shape or maintain a desirable height. The dense, elongated flower spikes are particularly attractive to bees. It can make a distinctive specimen, especially for the back of a garden.

Butterflies, bees, and other insect pollinators; it serves as a larval host for the southern dogface (Zerene cesonia) and the silver-spotted skipper (Epargryeus clarus).

Foxglove Penstemon

Scientific Name *Penstemon digitalis*

Family Plantaginaceae

Plant Characteristics Upright perennial 2–5 feet in height; basal leaves are shiny and dark green to purple-green; tubular flowers have white lobes and grow in branching clusters borne on sturdy stems with tall leaves.

USDA Hardiness Zones 3a–7b

Bloom Period Late spring–summer (May–July)

Growing Conditions Full sun or partial shade and dry-to-moist, well-drained soil.

This lovely native plant is common in prairies, moist open woodlands, forest edges, and along streams, as well as disturbed sites across much of the region. It is highly adaptable to a variety of garden soils and light conditions but flourishes in sunny locations with consistent moisture. Nonetheless, once established, it is tolerant of heat and drought. Foxglove penstemon is a clump-forming plant that boasts attractive, glossy-green leaves that are often tinged with red or purple. The real show, however, starts early in the season with the production of tall flower stalks that support a profuse array of white tubular blossoms. The resulting abundant forage resources are highly enticing to many pollinators and help make this perennial a choice selection for any wildlife garden.

Particularly attractive to butterflies, sphinx moths, bees, and hummingbirds.

Golden Alexanders

Scientific Name *Zizia aurea*

Family Apiaceae

Plant Characteristics Herbaceous perennial 1–3 feet in height; leaves are shiny, dark green, and compound, with variable leaflet size and shape; tiny yellow flowers grow in broad flat clusters.

USDA Hardiness Zones 3a–7b

Bloom Period Spring–summer (April–June)

Growing Conditions Full sun or partial shade and somewhat moist, well-drained soil.

Golden Alexanders bloom for a relatively long period in spring, adding some needed early-season cheer and interest to the landscape. The plant's broad, airy golden-yellow flower clusters pop against the contrasting profusion of dark-green glossy leaves and are a magnet for a wide range of smaller pollinators and beneficial insects. It thrives in bright, moist sites and is a great addition to wet meadows and prairies, open woodlands, or rain and wildlife gardens. Although plants tend to be somewhat short-lived, they readily reseed and often form small, low-growing colonies.

Butterflies, bees, and other insect pollinators; this attractive member of the carrot family serves as an important native larval host for the eastern black swallowtail (Papilio polyxenes).

Great Blue Lobelia

Scientific Name *Lobelia siphilitica*

Family Campanulaceae

Plant Characteristics Upright herbaceous perennial 2–4 feet in height; green leaves are elliptical and toothed; two-lipped tubular flowers are bright blue and grow on tall, terminal spikes borne on sturdy, tall green stems.

USDA Hardiness Zones 4a–7b

Bloom Period Summer–fall (July–September)

Growing Conditions Performs best in full sun to partial shade and fertile, moist-to-wet soil.

This distinctive perennial provides a pop of brilliant blue to the late-season landscape. Excellent for naturalizing or in a perennial border, the clump-forming plants flourish in moist, organically rich soil and varying levels of sunlight and shade. As a result, they are an eye-catching addition to any woodland garden. Great blue lobelia is easy to grow and requires little maintenance, but it is intolerant of drought. The flashy spires of flaring, bell-shaped blooms are regularly visited by bees, butterflies, and hummingbirds. Flower color often varies somewhat from light blue to a dark, deep blue. Plants freely self-seed and often spread to form larger colonies.

Highly attractive to butterflies, bees, and many other insect pollinators, as well as hummingbirds.

187

Halberd-leaf Rosemallow

Scientific Name *Hibiscus laevis*

Family Malvaceae

Plant Characteristics Stout, upright, and sparingly branched herbaceous perennial 3–6 feet in height; large green leaves have 3–5 lobes; broad flowers consist of 5 pale pink petals surrounding a darker center.

USDA Hardiness Zones 4a–7b

Bloom Period Midsummer–early fall (August–September)

Growing Conditions Full sun to partial shade and moist-to-wet soil; adapts well to organically rich, regularly moist garden soil, but intolerant of dry conditions and drought.

This handsome wetland perennial is typically found in or along marshes, swamps, ponds, rivers, and streams. The stout, upright stems are occasionally branched and support sizable leaves that are often three-lobed. This distinctive shape resembles a halberd, a long pole weapon consisting of an ax blade and a spear tip that was common in the fourteenth to sixteenth centuries. Occasionally, leaves may have up to five lobes. The large flowers are particularly showy and range from pale pink to nearly white with noticeably deep-pink-to-reddish centers. While tolerant of some shade, they flower the most when in full sun. Halberd-leaf rosemallow attracts a range of pollinating insects and hummingbirds. It is ideal for rain gardens, stream or pond margins, or for use in low, perpetually moist landscape sites.

Attractive to butterflies, bees, and hummingbirds; it serves as a larval host plant for the gray hairstreak (Strymon melinus), *checkered skipper* (Pyrgus communis), *and painted lady* (Vanessa cardui) *butterflies.*

Maryland Senna

Scientific Name *Senna marilandica*

Family Fabaceae

Plant Characteristics Shrubby upright herbaceous perennial 3–6 feet in height; compound green leaves are long and ferny; pea-like flowers are bright yellow and grow in both terminal and axillary clusters.

USDA Hardiness Zones 4a–7b

Bloom Period Summer (July–August)

Growing Conditions Full sun to partial light shade and a variety of average-to-moist, well-drained soils; adapts well to a variety of garden soils.

With its airy, large, locust-like leaves, this stately perennial adds a distinctive softness and texture to the landscape. Highly attractive individually or in smaller groups, it is an easy plant to grow, highly adaptable to a variety of well-drained soils, and tolerant of increased summer heat and humidity. Maryland senna is a pleasing addition to any native garden, prairie, or meadow, or the back of a perennial border. Beginning in midsummer, plants begin producing showy clusters of golden-yellow flowers that are frequently visited by bumblebees and other native bees. Each leaf petiole also possesses a nectar-producing gland outside the flower (these are known as extrafloral nectaries) at its base that attracts a wide variety of other beneficial insects, including ants, flies, and wasps. The copious blooms are quickly replaced by elongated, pendulous bean-like seedpods. The resulting seed is a valuable food source for various game birds, such as quail, and other wildlife.

*Bees and other insect pollinators; it serves as a larval host for the cloudless sulphur (*Phoebis sennae*) and sleepy orange (*Abaeis nicippe*) butterflies.*

Michigan Lily

Scientific Name *Lilium michiganense*

Family Liliaceae

Plant Characteristics Upright herbaceous perennial 2–5 feet in height; smooth, elliptical green leaves grow in staggered whorls along a central, unbranched green stem; one to many terminal, nodding, dark-spotted orange flowers grow on long stalks.

USDA Hardiness Zones 3a–7b

Bloom Period Summer (June–August)

Growing Conditions Performs best in full sun or partial shade and fertile, moist-to-wet, well-drained soil.

When in full bloom, it is hard to imagine a more exquisite wildflower. It is widespread in wet meadows and prairies, moist slopes, and open deciduous woodlands. Despite being highly ornamental and easy to grow, Michigan lily is highly underutilized. Thriving in organically rich soil with consistent moisture, it is a wonderful addition to perennial borders, rain and cottage gardens, or for naturalizing in larger, open landscapes or along ponds. It's best planted in groupings or en masse for the most eye-catching effect. Well-established plants can tolerate temporary drought. Plants have graceful, sturdy stems that give rise to nodding, bright orange flowers with highly recurved spotted petals and long, protruding anthers.

Highly attractive to butterflies, sphinx moths, and hummingbirds.

New Jersey Tea

Scientific Name *Ceanothus americanus*

Family Rhamnaceae

Plant Characteristics Upright deciduous shrub to 3 feet tall or more and just as wide; leaves are broad and green; small, white flowers grow in dense rounded clusters.

USDA Hardiness Zones 4a–7b

Bloom Period Summer (June–August)

Growing Conditions Full sun or partial shade and average-to-dry, well-drained soil.

This charming native has a compact and somewhat rounded growth habit. Considered a sub-shrub, it may die back to the ground in winter, especially when young, but it becomes more woody with age. It thrives in sunny locations with average moisture levels, but it can adapt to poor soil and is drought tolerant once established. It is a great addition to any native garden, especially when used at the back of a perennial border, along woodland edges, or on rocky slopes. New Jersey tea produces a profusion of delicate, somewhat fuzzy-looking, rounded pure-white flower heads that are a true favorite for pollinators.

Butterflies, bees, and other insect pollinators, as well as humming-birds. New Jersey tea is a larval host for the mottled duskywing (Erynnis martialis), summer azure (Celastrina neglecta), and spring azure (Celastrina ladon) butterflies.

195

Northern Spicebush

Scientific Name *Lindera benzoin*

Family Lauraceae

Plant Characteristics Deciduous shrub to 12 feet in
height or more; leaves are large, dark green, and
elliptical; tiny yellow flowers grow in small clusters
along the branches.

USDA Hardiness Zones 4a–7b

Bloom Period Spring (March–April)

Growing Conditions Full sun or partial shade and moist,
well-drained soil.

This is an attractive, multi-stemmed shrub found in rich, moist
woodlands. Plants have a rounded, open growth habit and can be
quite ornamental. In early spring, the bare, speckled branches burst
forth with a profusion of small yellow flower clusters. Although not
showy, the fragrant blooms attract a variety of insect pollinators.
They are quickly replaced by smooth, green leaves that are quite aromatic when crushed, providing this native with its distinctive name.

*Butterflies, bees, flies, and other pollinators; serves as a host for
the spicebush swallowtail butterfly (Papilio troilus).*

Obedient Plant

Scientific Name *Physostegia virginiana*

Family Lamiaceae

Plant Characteristics Upright herbaceous perennial 3–4 feet in height or more; toothed green leaves are elongated and lance-shaped; tubular, two-lipped flowers are pink to purple and grow in dense spikes borne on sturdy erect stems.

USDA Hardiness Zones 3a–7b

Bloom Period Summer to early fall (July–September)

Growing Conditions Performs best in full sun to partial shade and rich, average-to-moist, well-drained soil.

A showy and somewhat underused native, it is a plant of moist meadows, bogs, stream margins, and wetland borders. While an excellent addition to these natural landscapes, especially en masse, obedient plant is also easy to grow in rich garden soil with regular irrigation; it does not perform well in poor, dry soil and is relatively intolerant of drought. Mature plants tend to flop a bit and often require staking. It can spread somewhat aggressively by seed or underground rhizomes and may require some maintenance or division to keep in check. A late-season bloomer, it produces impressive spires of large, snapdragon-like flowers that are regularly visited by bees, butterflies, and hummingbirds. Several commercial cultivars are available, including those that are more compact or flower in white.

Particularly attractive to butterflies, sphinx moths, bees, and hummingbirds.

Ohio Spiderwort

Scientific Name *Tradescantia ohiensis*

Family Commelinaceae

Plant Characteristics Clump-forming upright herbaceous perennial 2–3 feet in height and about as wide; leaves are grass-like; bright flower clusters are dark blue to violet.

USDA Hardiness Zones 4a–7b

Bloom Period Spring to early summer (May–July)

Growing Conditions Prospers in full sun but is highly adaptable to partial shade and a variety of dry-to-moist, well-drained soils; benefits from extra moisture but is tolerant of drought once established.

This low-maintenance early-season native wildflower is underused as a landscape plant. Its distinctive linear foliage adds interest and soft texture, and the colorful blooms are a magnet for bees. The noticeably bright-yellow anthers appear to almost hover above each blossom and provide an abundance of high-quality pollen. Although it blooms for a relatively long period, individual flowers last only one day and often close-up by midday. Highly adaptable to a variety of light and soil conditions, it is a unique addition to a perennial border, woodland, cottage garden, or wildflower meadow. Ohio spiderwort excels in rich soil with consistent moisture and is capable of forming large, rounded clumps. Its overall appearance can become a bit untidy as the summer progresses, so combine it with a variety of attractive companion plants, such as pink swamp milkweed (page 207), common boneset (page 169), and black-eyed Susan (page 43) for the best results, or cut back to encourage regrowth. Spiderwort may aggressively self-seed; it is deer resistant.

Particularly attractive to bees.

Partridge Pea

Scientific Name *Chamaecrista fasciculata*

Family Fabaceae

Plant Characteristics Upright to sprawling herbaceous annual 1–3 feet in height; green leaves are compound, each with numerous oblong leaflets; large, butter-yellow irregular flowers are borne on reddish green stems.

USDA Hardiness Zones 3a–7b

Bloom Period Summer–fall (July–September)

Growing Conditions Performs best in full sun to partial shade and average-to-dry, well-drained soil.

An early colonizer of open, disturbed sites, partridge pea offers tremendous wildlife value, and its beauty as a landscape plant is often underappreciated. This durable annual tolerates poor growing conditions, establishes rapidly, and helps fix atmospheric nitrogen into the soil. As a result, it is excellent for naturalizing larger areas and is frequently used to stabilize slopes and prevent erosion. Plants have an airy, fern-like appearance that adds soft texture to the landscape and cover for wildlife. Individual leaves are somewhat sensitive to touch and tend to close up when disturbed. They also close up during the heat of day to conserve moisture. The petioles possess nectar-producing glands (extrafloral nectaries) that attract ants, wasps, and other highly beneficial insects. Plants produce copious amounts of seed and freely self-sow. The resulting seed is an important food source for many songbirds, turkeys, quail, pheasants, and ducks, as well as small mammals.

Butterflies, bees, and other insect pollinators; several butterflies, including the gray hairstreak (Strymon melinus), cloudless sulphur (Phoebis sennae), and little yellow (Pyrisitia lisa), use the plant as a larval host; the showy yellow flowers are particularly attractive to bees.

Pawpaw

Scientific Name *Asimina triloba*

Family Annonaceae

Plant Characteristics Small deciduous tree to 30 feet in height; leaves are large, oval, and shiny green; nodding leathery flowers are reddish brown and grow on short stalks from the branches.

USDA Hardiness Zones 5a–7b

Bloom Period Spring (April–May)

Growing Conditions Full sun or partial shade and fertile, moist, well-drained soil.

A common tree in southern portions of the region, pawpaw is easy to grow in moist, rich soil. It is a good addition to a woodland garden, forest margin, or when planted in the understory of larger trees. In spring, just as leaves are emerging, branches produce highly distinctive nodding flowers. The reddish brown blooms are fleshy in appearance and heavily veined, and they produce a mild fragrance of rotting carrion. The putrid aroma attracts an assortment of flies, which pollinate the flowers. The flowers are followed by large, shiny leaves and eventually develop into large, oblong edible fruit. While not a flashy plant, it is a great choice for a wildlife garden or for naturalizing in or near wooded landscapes.

Butterflies, bees, flies, and other pollinators; serves as a host for the extremely showy zebra swallowtail butterfly (Eurytides marcellus).

Pink Swamp Milkweed

Scientific Name *Asclepias incarnata*

Family Apocynaceae

Plant Characteristics Tall upright herbaceous perennial 3–5 feet in height; leaves are narrow and green; fragrant flowers are light pink to rose-colored and grow in tight flat clusters atop branched stems. Pink swamp milkweed forms relatively dense clumps over time.

USDA Hardiness Zones 3a–7b

Bloom Period Summer (July–September)

Growing Conditions Full sun or light shade and moist-to-saturated soil; adaptable to a range of garden soils if regular irrigation is available.

This moisture-loving native is yet another landscape-worthy milkweed. It is common in marshes, wet roadside ditches, and moist prairies throughout the region. A graceful, branched perennial, pink swamp milkweed is an excellent addition to a water garden, sunny wetland margin, or any wet area of a yard. It also adds height and interest when incorporated into a container garden. It is widely used by monarchs as a larval host, and the delicate blooms attract a myriad of insect pollinators. Easy to grow from seed, it requires little care once established. It is one of the most commonly available milkweed species commercially. The popular cultivar "Ice Ballet" has elegant pure-white flowers and foliage of a somewhat darker green.

Very attractive to butterflies, bees, and other insect pollinators, as well as hummingbirds; it is famous as a larval host for monarch butterflies.

Purple Passionflower

Scientific Name *Passiflora incarnata*

Family Passifloraceae

Plant Characteristics Perennial twining vine to 15 feet or more in length; large leaves are dark green and have three lobes; solitary lavender flowers are large and highly intricate.

USDA Hardiness Zones 5a–7b

Bloom Period Spring–summer (May–June)

Growing Conditions Full sun or partial shade, average moisture, and well-drained soil.

Native to the southernmost portions of the Midwest, from southern Missouri to Ohio, it can be grown farther north but is not reliably hardy. Purple passionflower is best planted in a protected area to buffer it from harsh winter temperatures. It is a fast-growing twining, spreading vine that can be easily trained up a trellis or grown along the ground. Highly ornamental, the vine features dark-green foliage and sizable, eye-catching fringed flowers that draw in bees, butterflies, and other insect pollinators. It spreads by root suckers, forming small colonies. Also called maypop, plants produce a large, rounded fruit with edible pulp; a different species of passionflower, found in South America, produces the passion fruit.

Butterflies, bees, flies, and other pollinators; serves as a larval host for the variegated fritillary butterfly (Euptoieta claudia).

Purplestem Angelica

Scientific Name *Angelica atropurpurea*

Family Apiaceae

Plant Characteristics Stout upright herbaceous perennial 3–8 feet or more in height; large green leaves are compound, with several toothed oval leaflets; large domed clusters of numerous tiny, greenish white flowers are borne on tall, purplish hollow stems.

USDA Hardiness Zones 4a–7b

Bloom Period Spring–summer (May–June)

Growing Conditions Performs best in full sun to light shade and moist, well-drained, organically rich soil.

An impressive plant in form and in stature, purplestem angelica ranks among the tallest wildflowers in the region. The lower portions of the plant are adorned with compound, somewhat ferny-looking leaves that can approach two feet in length. As its name suggests, the plant's sturdy, soaring stems are tinged with purple, providing a lovely accent to its darker-green foliage. Starting in late spring, plants produce tall stalks that render broad, umbrella-like flower heads many inches across. The tiny whitish flowers attract a myriad of smaller insect pollinators. A wetland species found in marshes and soggy meadows, along streams, or in wet ditches, it thrives in sites with dappled shade and consistent moisture, and it can even tolerate regular inundation. Perfect for natural landscapes, or as a specimen in a rain or wildlife garden.

Butterflies, bees, and other insect pollinators; it serves as a larval host for the eastern black swallowtail butterfly (Papilio polyxenes).

Pussy Willow

Scientific Name *Salix discolor*

Family Salicaceae

Plant Characteristics Deciduous shrub 10–25 feet in height; leaves are stiff, dark green, and oval; silky catkins (flowering spikes) are produced on bare stems.

USDA Hardiness Zones 4a–7b

Bloom Period Spring (March–April)

Growing Conditions Performs best in full sun to partial shade and moist-to-wet soil.

A true harbinger of spring, this familiar shrub is well known for its distinctive and highly ornamental fuzzy catkins that appear on bare branches well before the leaves emerge. It is a dioecious species, which means that each plant produces either male or female flowers. While both are attractive, the male blooms represent the traditional downy-gray catkins that are most frequently pictured or commonly sold with early-season floral bouquets. They soon begin to open, showcasing an abundance of yellow stamens that offer a great early-season pollen source for bees. With a strongly upright growth habit, pussy willow boasts leaves that are noticeably silvery beneath, giving the plants an overall grayish green appearance. Best grown in wet areas, it tends to sucker readily from the roots and can form dense stands over time.

Butterflies, bees, and other insect pollinators; it serves as a larval host for several butterflies, including the Acadian hairstreak (Strymon acadica), *mourning cloak* (Nymphalis antiopa), *and viceroy* (Limenitis archippus).

213

Red Maple

Scientific Name *Acer rubrum*

Family Sapindaceae

Plant Characteristics Deciduous tree to 70 feet or more in height; broad green leaves have 3–5 lobes and toothed margins and grow on long red stems; small, red flowers grow in clusters.

USDA Hardiness Zones 3a–7b

Bloom Period Spring (March–April)

Growing Conditions Full sun or partial shade and moist, well-drained soil.

Aptly named, this attractive tree sports flashes of red throughout the growing season. Starting in early spring, it produces clusters of small, red flowers, which offer bees an abundant source of nutrient-rich pollen and nectar before many other plants are even in bloom. Hanging red-tinged winged seeds and young leaves soon follow. The traditional palm-shaped leaves quickly mature to dark green with a lighter green-gray underside. The real show, though, occurs in autumn, when the foliage bursts into a brilliant red. The exact fall color can vary slightly between trees. Red maple is a vigorous grower and quite adaptable; it thrives in moist conditions and can even tolerate temporary inundation. Highly ornamental, it is great for wild spaces or as a showcase tree. Several commercial cultivars are available.

Bees; it is a larval host for the rosy maple moth, the io moth, and the cecropia moth.

Royal Catchfly

Scientific Name *Silene regia*

Family Caryophyllaceae

Plant Characteristics Upright herbaceous perennial
2–4 feet in height; leaves are long, lance-shaped, and
light green; tubular bright-red flowers each have five
prominent petals and grow in terminal clusters.

USDA Hardiness Zones 4a–7b

Bloom Period Summer (July–August)

Growing Conditions Performs best in full sun to partial
shade and average-to-dry, well-drained soil.

Extremely well named, this majestic species boasts brilliant cardinal-
red flowers truly deserving of royalty. The tall clusters of large, star-
shaped blooms invite accolades from onlookers along with frequent
visits by larger butterflies and ruby-throated hummingbirds. As red
is a generally uncommon color, royal catchfly is particularly stunning
en masse and when planted alongside the more customary purples
and yellows of the late-season landscape. While generally easy to
grow in well-drained, sunny locations, plants may take several years
to fully establish. It is a good choice for rocky or gravelly sites. This
wildflower is rare and listed as threatened or endangered in several
states, but it is increasingly sold commercially, especially through
native plant nurseries.

Butterflies and hummingbirds.

Sassafras

Scientific Name *Sassafras albidum*

Family Lauraceae

Plant Characteristics Deciduous tree 20–40 feet in height or more; large leaves are bright green and have two or three lobes; tiny yellow flowers grow in small clusters at the branch tips.

USDA Hardiness Zones 4a–7b

Bloom Period Spring (April–May)

Growing Conditions Full sun or partial shade, average moisture, and well-drained soil.

Although generally a small- to medium-sized pioneer tree (a tree that is first to colonize an environment), some specimens have staying power and can reach heights approaching 80 feet. It spreads by suckering and can often form dense stands. Sassafras is an excellent addition to any butterfly or wildlife garden, open woodland, forest margin, or for naturalizing. The tiny spring blooms appear on bare branches. While not showy, they attract numerous flower-visiting insects. Large, very distinctive mitten-shaped leaves soon follow. While bright green during the growing season, they quickly transition to bold yellow or orange-red hues in autumn, providing a spectacular display of color. All parts of the plant are aromatic when crushed. Sassafras is the original "root" in traditionally made root beer.

Butterflies, bees, flies, and other pollinators; it is a favorite larval host of the spicebush swallowtail butterfly (Papilio troilus).

Scarlet Bee Balm

Scientific Name *Monarda didyma*

Family Lamiaceae

Plant Characteristics Coarse upright, clump-forming herbaceous perennial 2–4 feet in height; toothed leaves are dark green; dense rounded heads of brilliant red tubular flowers are borne atop sturdy square stems.

USDA Hardiness Zones 4a–7b

Bloom Period Summer (July–September)

Growing Conditions Full sun or partial shade and rich, moist soil.

Scarlet bee balm is highly ornamental and a true stunner when in bloom. As its name suggests, this perennial produces showy but somewhat raggedy rounded clusters of elongated brilliant red tubular flowers, with each head measuring up to 4 inches across. It is prolific and blooms for a relatively long period of time, staying productive for many weeks. Regular deadheading encourages more flower production. Like other members of the *Monarda* (bee balm) genus, it is adored by butterflies, hummingbirds, sphinx moths, and larger, long-tongued bees. It performs best in sunny locations with fertile garden soil and consistent moisture. Plants quickly expand in size and spread by both seed and underground rhizomes, forming colonies. It is susceptible to powdery mildew, a fungal infection that can occur, particularly during rainy periods or under crowded conditions that limit air circulation. That problem aside, scarlet bee balm is a stunning accent plant; cultivars of numerous colors are available commercially, including those in purple, yellow, and white. Highly powdery mildew-resistant varieties are available as well.

Particularly attractive to butterflies, sphinx moths, bees, and hummingbirds.

Spotted Bee Balm

Scientific Name *Monarda punctata*

Family Lamiaceae

Plant Characteristics Compact upright herbaceous perennial 1–3 feet in height; aromatic green leaves are narrow and toothed; rounded heads of pale-yellow tubular flowers are spotted with purple. Flower heads occur in several tiers up the sturdy square stem directly above a whorl of colorful cream-to-pink-colored bracts.

USDA Hardiness Zones 3a–7b

Bloom Period Midsummer–early fall (July–September)

Growing Conditions Full sun or partial shade and dry, well-drained sandy soil.

This somewhat obscure native bee balm also goes by the name dotted horsemint. A highly durable plant, it can tolerate poor soil and drought but benefits from consistent moisture in garden settings. Ideal for smaller landscapes or borders, it is a truly distinctive and somewhat untamed-looking addition. The dense clusters of small, two-lipped flowers appeal to a broad range of pollinators but are overshadowed by the more conspicuous and colorful bracts below. With each stem sporting several tiers of blooms, the overall appearance resembles a pagoda. Spotted bee balm plants are virtually maintenance-free and have a relatively long bloom period. A clump-forming perennial spotted bee balm can spread somewhat quickly by both seed and underground rhizomes.

Particularly attractive to butterflies, sphinx moths, bees, and hummingbirds.

Tall Green Milkweed

Scientific Name *Asclepias hirtella*

Family Apocynaceae

Plant Characteristics Narrow upright herbaceous perennial 2–4 feet in height; long, narrow green leaves are numerous; dense, showy round clusters of purple-spotted green flowers occur up the stem.

USDA Hardiness Zones 4b–7

Bloom Period Summer (June–August)

Growing Conditions Full sun or partial shade and dry-to-moderately wet soil; highly adaptable to a range of garden soils.

One of my absolute favorite milkweeds, this striking native prairie plant occurs across the region but is rare to uncommon throughout. In Michigan and Minnesota, it's listed as a threatened species. Despite its obscurity, seed is available commercially, and it's certainly a plant worth incorporating into any sunny pollinator or prairie garden. The slender, upright plants give rise to numerous flower clusters along the upper portion of the stem, each with copious amounts of individual flowers. When in full bloom, the plant is an absolute knockout and a highly interesting alternative to more-common milkweed species.

Attractive to butterflies, bees, moths, and other insect pollinators; tall green milkweed is regularly used by monarchs as a larval host.

White Turtlehead

Scientific Name *Chelone glabra*

Family Scrophulariaceae

Plant Characteristics Upright herbaceous perennial 2–4 feet in height; narrow lance-shaped leaves are dark green and serrated; cream-white two-lipped flowers grow in a terminal spike.

USDA Hardiness Zones 3a–7b

Bloom Period Summer–fall (July–September)

Growing Conditions Full sun or partial shade and moist-to-wet, fertile soil.

This clump-forming wetland species is typically encountered in wet meadows, fens, marshes, and along streams. It thrives in organically rich, moist soil and makes an attractive addition to natural landscapes as well as a showy accent in rain gardens, butterfly gardens, or perennial borders with consistent moisture. While it grows well in sun to partial shade, plants in lower-light environments often get scraggly and may require staking. White turtlehead is intolerant of dry conditions and drought. This plant gets its unique name from the distinctive, snapdragon-like flowers, the lower lip of which resembles a turtle's head sticking out from its shell. The dense, cream-to-pale-pink-infused flower clusters offer lovely late-season color and are frequently visited by bees and hummingbirds.

Bees, butterflies, and hummingbirds; it serves as a key larval host for the increasingly rare Baltimore checkerspot butterfly (Euphydryas phaeton).

White Wild Indigo

Scientific Name *Baptisia alba*

Family Fabaceae

Plant Characteristics Sturdy upright herbaceous perennial 2–5 feet in height or more; foliage is gray-green; pure-white, pea-like flowers grow in elongated spikes. It forms expanding multi-stemmed shrubby clumps over time.

USDA Hardiness Zones 4b–7b

Bloom Period Late spring–summer (May–July)

Growing Conditions Thrives in full sun or partial shade and a variety of dry-to-moist, well-drained, and slightly acidic soils.

This sturdy and easy-to-grow perennial adds to the landscape for much of the year. An early-season bloomer, the lovely immaculate white flowers are borne on long, graceful spires that may be over a foot in length and contrast wonderfully against the smoky-colored stems and darker foliage. The flower structure, color, and bloom period are well suited for bumblebees, which are not only exceedingly fond of the blossoms but represent the plant's primary pollinator. After flowering, white wild indigo produces rounded, inflated seedpods that turn dull black over time and further increase the visual appeal of this often underutilized native. Its shrubby, statuesque form provides an excellent backdrop to highlight smaller colorful companion species, such as black-eyed Susan (page 43), butterfly milkweed (page 49), and purple coneflower (page 103). Young plants are somewhat slow to establish and may take several years to flower. Over time though, they develop deep root systems and are quite drought tolerant and long-lived.

Particularly attractive to bumblebees; it may occasionally be used by the wild indigo duskywing (Erynnis baptisiae) as a larval host.

Wild Bergamot

Scientific Name *Monarda fistulosa*

Family Lamiaceae

Plant Characteristics Relatively compact upright herbaceous perennial 2–4 feet in height; leaves are light green; dense rounded heads of tubular light-pink flowers sit atop branched stems.

USDA Hardiness Zones 3a–7b

Bloom Period Midsummer–early fall (July–September)

Growing Conditions Full sun to partial shade and dry-to-somewhat moist, well-drained soil; adapts well to a variety of garden soils and is drought tolerant once established.

Also called bee balm, this widespread and relatively common colony-forming native is an excellent plant for pollinators. Butterflies and a broad range of other flower visitors adore this plant when it's in bloom. The individual powdery-pink-to-lavender tubular flowers form dense, somewhat raggedy heads atop stiff, branched square stems. Like many other members of the mint family, the leaves are also pleasantly aromatic when handled. A prolific bloomer and flowering for a relatively long period of time, wild bergamot thrives in sunny sites with rich soil and consistent moisture, but it can tolerate some shade. As a result, it is a great choice for a variety of landscape settings, including everything from herb gardens, perennial borders, and native gardens to larger meadows, open woodlands, and along forest margins. Combines well with common milkweed (page 53), purple coneflower (page 103), garden phlox (page 71), Virginia mountain mint (page 137), and yellow flowers such as black-eyed Susan (page 43) and yellow coneflower (page 149).

Particularly attractive to butterflies, sphinx moths, bees, and hummingbirds.

Wild Lupine

Scientific Name *Lupinus perennis*

Family Fabaceae

Plant Characteristics Compactly branched herbaceous perennial 1–2 feet in height; leaves are green and palm-like; upright spikes of violet-blue, pea-like flowers are produced on reddish green stalks.

USDA Hardiness Zones 3a–7b

Bloom Period Spring–Summer (May–June)

Growing Conditions Performs best in full sun to partial shade and average-to-dry, well-drained, sandy soil.

A graceful and underutilized wildflower, this spring ephemeral adds early-season beauty to any perennial garden or native landscape. Groupings or mass plantings provide a particularly stunning display when in full bloom, and flowers are soon followed by hairy, bean-like seedpods that provide continued visual interest. The slender, showy flower spikes attract an assortment of bees, butterflies, and other insect pollinators, as well as an occasional hummingbird. This species thrives in drier, sandy sites but is adaptable to other well-drained soil. Like other legumes, wild lupine enhances soil fertility by fixing atmospheric nitrogen into the soil. Plants spread by seed and underground rhizomes, forming larger colonies.

Butterflies, bees, and other insect pollinators; it is a larval host for numerous butterfly species, including the gray hairstreak (Strymon melinus), frosted elfin (Callophrys irus), wild indigo duskywing (Erynnis baptisiae), Persius duskywing (Erynnis persius), and the federally endangered Karner blue (Plebejus melissa samuelis).

Woolly Pipevine

Scientific Name *Aristolochia tomentosa*

Family Aristolochiaceae

Plant Characteristics Deciduous, climbing vine to 20 feet in height or more; leaves are large, dark green, and heart-shaped; distinctive but somewhat inconspicuous pipe-shaped flowers are yellow-green with a dark center.

USDA Hardiness Zones 5a–7b

Bloom Period Late spring–early summer (May–July)

Growing Conditions Full sun to partial shade and average-to-moist, well-drained soil; adapts well to organically rich garden soil; intolerant of dry conditions and drought.

Also called Dutchman's pipe, this lovely native perennial is a key larval host for the charismatic pipevine swallowtail butterfly, which is found in the southern part of our region. It is a fast-growing, twining vine that covers arbors, fences, and trellises, and ascends trees and other plants. Although typically encountered in moist woodlands, it is an essential addition to butterfly gardens in southern portions of the Midwest. The large, heart-shaped leaves are numerous, distinctive, and highly ornamental. The equally distinct flowers resemble the shape of a pipe but are smaller and often obscured by the dense foliage. They emit a putrid odor that readily attracts flies, their primary pollinators. As its name implies, all parts of the plant are noticeably hairy.

Attractive to butterflies and flies.

Wild Blue Phlox

Woodland Sunflower

Partial Shade to Full Shade

Cutleaf Coneflower

Purple Milkweed

Common Blue Violet

False Nettle

Virginia Bluebells

Red Columbine

From Virginia bluebells (page 253) to red columbine (page 249), some good wildlife-attracting plants prefer or can tolerate lower light levels. These plants often perform best with 3–6 hours of direct sunlight per day or less. In many cases, they benefit from some sun in the morning or evening when light intensity is reduced, but they are sensitive to too much sun. This can lead to increased stress, dehydration, even scorching. These plants are often best used along forest margins, under larger trees, in woodland gardens, or in north-facing border gardens.

Sweet Joe Pye Weed

Bigleaf Aster

Bigleaf Aster

Scientific Name *Eurybia macrophylla*

Family Asteraceae

Plant Characteristics Upright herbaceous perennial 1–2 feet in height; large, heart-shaped leaves are bright green with toothed margins; daisy-like flowers are white to light lavender with bright-yellow centers and grow in flat, terminal branched clusters.

USDA Hardiness Zones 3a–7b

Bloom Period Summer–fall (August–October)

Growing Conditions Performs best in partial sun to shade and organically rich, average-to-moist, well-drained soil.

A lovely wildflower common to woodlands and forest borders, bigleaf aster is a reliable choice for more dimly lit parts of the landscape, thriving best in dappled sunlight. While the plants grow well even in full shade, flower production is often limited. The plant's large heart-shaped leaves are quite distinctive and provide a wonderful backdrop to highlight the sparse flower heads and help brighten up darker corners of the garden. A wide variety of butterflies, bees, wasps, and other late-season pollinators flock to the blooms. Plants spread readily by underground rhizomes and form larger, dense colonies, serving as a highly attractive shade-loving groundcover.

Butterflies, bees, and other insect pollinators.

Common Blue Violet

Scientific Name *Viola sororia*

Family Violaceae

Plant Characteristics Herbaceous perennial 3–8 inches in height; broad green leaves are toothed and heart-shaped; flowers are small and violet-blue.

USDA Hardiness Zones 3a–7b

Bloom Period Spring–Summer (April–June)

Growing Conditions Performs best in partial shade and organically rich, moist, well-drained soil.

This cheery and diminutive species is a common wildflower of woodlands, moist slopes, and creek margins. While it prefers light-to-partial shade, common blue violet is often encountered in sunny wet meadows, prairies, and even shaded lawns in more-suburban locations. Exceptionally easy to grow and flexible when used in the landscape, it makes an excellent addition to any wooded garden or rain garden, when planted in containers on a patio, or as a showy groundcover. Plants freely self-seed and can spread quickly and even become a bit weedy. Individual flowers have five flaring violet-blue petals that are heavily striated at the throat and are displayed above the broad green leaves on slender stalks. While primarily a spring bloomer, flowers may periodically be produced throughout the growing season. Bees and other small insects occasionally visit the flowers.

Butterflies, bees, and other insect pollinators; serves as a larval host for numerous butterflies, including the Aphrodite fritillary (Speyeria aphrodite), the great spangled fritillary (Speyeria cybele), the variegated fritillary (Euptoieta claudia), and the meadow fritillary (Boloria bellona).

Cutleaf Coneflower

Scientific Name *Rudbeckia laciniata*

Family Asteraceae

Plant Characteristics Herbaceous perennial 3–4 feet in height or more; deeply lobed leaves are dark green; daisy-like flowers are yellow with a greenish center atop stiff, slender stems.

USDA Hardiness Zones 3a–7b

Bloom Period Summer–fall (late July–September)

Growing Conditions Performs best in partial shade and fertile, moist soil.

Typically encountered along forest margins, streams, and in wet meadows, this native moisture-loving perennial is intolerant of dry soil and drought. Forming sizable clumps, it can spread quickly via underground rhizomes and may be somewhat aggressive in the landscape. This growth habit makes cutleaf coneflower ideal for use in naturalizing or mass plantings. In smaller spaces, it is best used at the back of a perennial border; larger clumps can be occasionally divided to help control spread. The showy, bright-yellow flowers with drooping petals begin to appear on sturdy, upright stalks in mid- to late summer and continue through early fall. They are an absolute magnet for a wide range of pollinating insects. Spent flowers should be regularly deadheaded to encourage additional blooming. This species has few pest problems and is deer resistant. Several cultivars are available.

Highly attractive to butterflies, bees, and many other insect pollinators.

False Nettle

Scientific Name *Boehmeria cylindrica*

Family Urticaceae

Plant Characteristics Upright herbaceous perennial 1–3 feet in height; broad, prominently veined leaves are dark green and toothed; short spikes of small greenish flowers arise from leaf axils.

USDA Hardiness Zones 3b–7b

Bloom Period Summer (June–August)

Growing Conditions Partial shade and average-to-moist, well-drained soil.

While not grown for the beauty of its flowers, this moisture-loving native is a valuable addition to damp woodlands; stream; pond; or other wetland margins, or rain or butterfly gardens with lower light levels. Its preference for shadier locations provides gardeners with added flexibility, especially in spaces that don't receive full sunlight. Aptly named, false nettle closely resembles stinging nettle but lacks the unpleasant stinging hairs and is thus perfectly safe to handle. Although somewhat of a scraggly grower, plants can be easily shaped by occasional pruning to keep them more compact and bushy.

Butterflies, bees, and other insect pollinators; it serves as a larval host for the red admiral (Vanessa atalanta), question mark (Polygonia interrogationis), and the eastern comma (Polygonia comma) butterflies.

Purple Milkweed

Scientific Name *Asclepias purpurascens*

Family Apocynaceae

Plant Characteristics Tall upright herbaceous perennial 2–3 feet in height; large, oblong, pointed leaves are dark green with a central purplish vein; fragrant flowers are deep-pink to reddish purple and grow in showy rounded clusters.

USDA Hardiness Zones 4a–7b

Bloom Period Summer (June–July)

Growing Conditions Partial shade and average-to-moist, well-drained soil.

With its large clusters of deeply rose-colored flowers, this milkweed is a showstopper. The ample blooms are a magnet for butterflies, bees, sphinx moths, and other insect pollinators, as well as hummingbirds. Although similar in appearance and stature to common milkweed (page 53), it is not nearly as aggressive. Nonetheless, it does still spread by underground rhizomes and can form larger colonies over time. While purple milkweed prefers richer, moist soil and often grows best in a bit of light or dappled shade, it is highly adaptable and can perform well in full sun and tolerate drought once established. Its ornamental nature makes this species a great addition to any wildlife garden or perennial border, as well as a larger meadow or woodland border. After flowering, the plants produce smooth, narrow seed pods that eventually burst open to release the silk-laden seeds.

Very attractive to butterflies, bees, and other insect pollinators, as well as hummingbirds.

Red Columbine

Scientific Name *Aquilegia canadensis*

Family Ranunculaceae

Plant Characteristics Graceful upright herbaceous perennial 1–3 feet in height; leaves are airy, compound, and lobed; showy bell-shaped, nodding flowers are red and yellow and bear long spurs.

USDA Hardiness Zones 3b–7b

Bloom Period Late spring (April–June)

Growing Conditions Partial shade and average-to-moist, well-drained soil.

This lovely native wildflower adds beauty and texture to any spring landscape. The compact plant boasts delicate, ferny foliage and distinctive red pendulous flowers with yellow centers; the flowers are supported on upright, branched stalks. Each flower has five long curved nectar spurs. Wild columbine is easy to grow and highly adaptable to a variety of well-drained garden soils and light conditions, from full sun to moderate shade. An early bloomer, the flowers are a favorite of hummingbirds and many bees at a time, and flowers occur in late spring, when forage resources are often limited. It is an excellent choice for woodland, shade, and cottage gardens, especially when combined with other colorful spring species such as wild blue phlox (page 257) and white wild indigo (page 229). It is equally ideal for naturalizing. It is generally resistant to damage from deer and rabbits.

Very attractive to hummingbirds, butterflies, sphinx moths, and bees; the plant serves as a larval host for the columbine duskywing (Erynnis lucilius).

Sweet Joe Pye Weed

Scientific Name *Eutrochium purpureum*

Family Asteraceae

Plant Characteristics Upright herbaceous perennial 4–7 feet in height or more; highly textured, toothed green leaves occur in whorls spaced out along a sturdy green stem; fuzzy pinkish flowers grow in large, rounded terminal clusters.

USDA Hardiness Zones 4a–7b

Bloom Period Summer–fall (July–September)

Growing Conditions Performs best in partial shade and fertile, moist, well-drained soil.

This is a robust and stately wildflower of open woodlands and forest borders. Unlike many pollinator favorites, sweet Joe Pye weed performs well across everything from full sun to considerable shade, making it a highly flexible landscape addition. The towering plants thrive in moist, organically rich soil and expand into sizable multi-stemmed clumps over time. The domed terminal clusters of fragrant, vanilla-scented pale-purple flowers are virtually irresistible to butterflies, moths, and bees. Established plants are equally striking individually or en masse, providing a wonderful combination of height, texture, and color. Several showy cultivars are available that are well suited for gardens. For details on its odd name, see page 125.

Highly attractive to butterflies, bees, and many other insect pollinators.

Virginia Bluebells

Scientific Name *Mertensia virginica*

Family Boraginaceae

Plant Characteristics Upright herbaceous perennial 1–2 feet in height; leaves are gray-green and oval; pendulous tubular flowers are light blue and grow in terminal clusters.

USDA Hardiness Zones 3a– 7b

Bloom Period Spring (April–May)

Growing Conditions Performs best in partial to full shade and organically rich, moist, well-drained soil.

This is a lovely spring wildflower of moist woodlands and stream or creek margins, often blooming before most trees have fully leafed out. It thrives in moist, fertile soil and grows best in shadier portions of the landscape. A clump-forming perennial, it can often form sizable colonies over time under optimal growing conditions. The large light-colored leaves have a soft, floppy appearance and help brighten the understory. They also provide an excellent backdrop for the showy trumpet-shaped flowers. Each bud starts out pinkish before soon transforming into the characteristic light-blue color at maturity. True to its name, its dangling flower clusters do resemble miniature bells. Flowers are regularly visited by bees, butterflies, and sphinx moths. Plants have a relatively long blooming period before dying back to the ground by midsummer. Virginia bluebell provide early-season interest and color to any woodland garden or shadier perennial border. It is also an exceptional species for naturalizing larger areas.

Butterflies, bees, and other insect pollinators.

Virginia Snakeroot

Scientific Name *Aristolochia serpentaria*

Family Aristolochiaceae

Plant Characteristics Herbaceous perennial 6 inches to 2 feet in height; green leaves are heart-shaped to narrow and spear-shaped; small, purplish brown, pipe-shaped flowers grow near the base of the plant.

USDA Hardiness Zones 5a–7b

Bloom Period Spring–summer (May–June)

Growing Conditions Full shade and rich, moist, well-drained soil.

This dainty and diminutive perennial is widespread in rich woodlands across southern portions of the region, although you may have to look closely to find it. Plants have an ascending growth habit and a distinctive thin zigzagging stem. Like other members of the genus, the leaves are somewhat heart-shaped but vary greatly in width from very narrow to more broad. The distinctive pipe-shaped flowers occur low near the ground and often bloom below the leaf litter. They are pollinated by flies and gnats. Plants spread via rhizomes and form small colonies along the forest floor. It is an ideal species for a woodland or shady area or a butterfly garden. Native to the Appalachians and the southern portion of our region, woolly pipevine (page 235) is a much larger twining vine that can be grown in more-southern portions of the region.

Butterflies; Virginia snakeroot serves as the larval host for the flashy pipevine swallowtail butterfly (Battus philenor); its larvae require multiple plants to complete development.

Wild Blue Phlox

Scientific Name *Phlox divaricata*

Family Fabaceae

Plant Characteristics Herbaceous mounding perennial to 1–1.5 feet in height; green leaves are elliptical to lance-shaped; fragrant flowers range in color from lilac to light blue and grow in somewhat flat clusters.

USDA Hardiness Zones 3a–7b

Bloom Period Spring–summer (April–June)

Growing Conditions Performs best in partial shade and rich, moist, well-drained sandy soil.

Wild blue phlox is a lovely spring ephemeral wildflower that forms foot-tall clumps. Plants have semi-evergreen oval or lance-shaped deep-green leaves. In early spring, foliage is crowned by loose clusters of showy pinkish lavender or icy blue flowers. It is a fine ground-cover for woodlands or shade gardens with moist well-drained soil. Wild blue phlox makes an excellent addition to a perennial border, a naturalized area, or a rock garden.

Butterflies, bees, and other insect pollinators.

Woodland Sunflower

Scientific Name *Helianthus divaricatus*

Family Asteraceae

Plant Characteristics Upright herbaceous perennial 3–6 feet in height; yellow-green leaves are lance-shaped and taper to a short point; large terminal flowers are bright yellow atop stiff reddish brown stems.

USDA Hardiness Zones 3a–7b

Bloom Period Summer–fall (July–September)

Growing Conditions Performs best in partial shade and average-to-dry, well-drained soil.

As its name suggests, this is a widespread and common wildflower of dry, open woodlands, forest clearings, and forest borders. The stiff, slender stems boast rough yellow-green leaves and add both height and texture to shadier areas of the landscape. In late summer, the statuesque plants begin producing numerous golden flowers that brighten wooded sites or nearby meadows. The attractive characteristic sunflower blooms are frequently visited by a variety of insect pollinators. Woodland sunflower spreads vigorously via underground rhizomes and expands into sizable colonies, making the species useful for naturalizing. Its aggressive nature can quickly overwhelm smaller garden spaces.

Butterflies, bees, and other insect pollinators; serves as a larval host for the gorgone checkerspot (Chlosyne gorgone) *and silvery checkerspot* (Chlosyne nycteis) *butterflies.*

Garden Design for Butterflies

garden Design for Bees

Garden Container for Pollinators

3

4

5

Building a Bee Box

The vast majority of native bees are solitary and non-aggressive. They are highly beneficial, fun to observe, and easy to attract. Beyond the floral resources that they depend upon for food in the form of nectar and pollen, native bees also require nest sites. Many native bees actually nest in the ground. The female bee excavates individual subterranean tunnels, each with many chambers, and provisions them with pollen for the developing young to eat. Once outfitted with sufficient resources, she moves on, and her young develop on their own with no additional maternal care. Other native bees seek out existing structures. They prefer to nest in small tunnels, such as hollow stems or the holes left behind from wood-boring beetles. For these species, dead wood and vegetation, snags, and brush piles are often prime nesting sites. If such resources are limited or undesirable in the landscape, many of these same tunnel-nesting species can be attracted with artificial nest boxes. Such nest boxes are not intended to replace natural nesting habitat but simply help augment them. They may also help boost local bee populations. Nest boxes are widely available at many commercial outlets, including garden centers, nature stores, and various online retailers. However, they are also quite easy to construct, with little investment of time or money. Later, these basic structures can also be expanded into larger bee "hotels" that offer added nesting opportunities as well as visual interest to the landscape. Some can be true works of art.

There are two main ways to build a bee house—with wooden blocks or stem bundles.

BUILDING A WOODEN BLOCK NEST

- One or more blocks of natural, untreated wood (ideally 4" wide and 6" deep, and heights of 6" to 18" or larger)

- If large blocks of wood are unavailable, several pieces of lumber can be glued together to achieve the appropriate dimensions.

- Alternatively, larger dead branches or logs can be cut into shorter sections and used.

- An electric drill, with multiple drill bits of various diameters from ¼" to about ⅜"

- Bracket for mounting or hanging

Place the wooden block on the ground or workbench. Using the various-diameter bits, drill into the block on one side, starting about 1" from each edge. For branches or logs, drill into the flat cut end. Be sure to drill straight into the block and avoid angled holes. Aim for a hole depth at of at least 3–6", but be careful to not drill completely through the block. Once you have one hole drilled, change your drill bit, and drill another hole about 1" away. Continue drilling holes, and changing drill bits, until the block is fully drilled. Then secure the bracket on the top or back of the block and mount firmly on a building, fence post, tree, or other structure in a protected location with morning sun. The same technique can be used to drill various-diameter holes into a dead stump.

BUILDING A STEM BUNDLE NEST

Supplies

- Even-length bundles of reeds*, bamboo*, hollow stems, or paper straws

- Wire or zip tie

Take a handful of variously sized materials and strap them together in a very tight bundle using the wire or plastic zip tie. Depending on size, one or more bundles can then be placed open-end out in a variety of containers, such as a wood-frame box, a hollowed out branch, or a piece of PVC pipe with a cap at one end. The resulting container should be placed in a sheltered location with morning sun, several feet off the ground, and with the bundles perpendicular to the ground. There are a wide range of potential designs.

Whichever design you choose, please note that wooden blocks and stem bundles can deteriorate quickly under outdoor conditions and should be replaced every few years for best results and to minimize adverse impacts on native bee health.

Note*: If using bamboo or reeds, be sure to cut each piece below a node to ensure that one end is open and the other is closed; additionally, you may need to drill out some of the material to acquire the desired range of hole sizes. If using straws, place the bundles flush against the structure, so one end is open, and the other closed.

Bird Food or Nesting Plants

COMMON NAME	SCIENTIFIC NAME
Big Bluestem pg. 41	*Andropogon gerardii*
Black-eyed Susan pg. 43	*Rudbeckia hirta*
Common Ironweed pg. 51	*Vernonia fasciculata*
Common Ninebark pg. 55	*Physocarpus opulifolius*
Cup Plant pg. 65	*Silphium perfoliatum*
Indian Blanket pg. 75	*Gaillardia pulchella*
Lanceleaf Coreopsis pg. 77	*Coreopsis lanceolata*
Leadplant pg. 81	*Amorpha canescens*
Little Bluestem pg. 83	*Schizachyrium scoparium*
Meadowsweet pg. 89	*Spiraea alba*
New England Aster pg. 91	*Symphyotrichum novae–angliae*
Orange Coneflower pg. 97	*Rudbeckia fulgida*
Pale Purple Coneflower, pg. 103	*Echinacea pallida*
Possumhaw, pg. 147	*Ilex decidua*
Prairie Dock pg. 101	*Silphium terebinthinaceum*
Purple Coneflower pg. 103	*Echinacea purpurea*
Roughleaf Dogwood pg. 113	*Cornus drummondii*
Sky Blue Aster pg. 121	*Symphyotrichum oolentangiense*
Staghorn Sumac pg. 127	*Rhus typhina*
Western Sunflower pg. 141	*Helianthus occidentalis*
Winterberry pg. 147	*Ilex verticillata*
Yellow Coneflower pg. 149	*Ratibida pinnata*

COMMON NAME	SCIENTIFIC NAME
American Basswood pg. 153	*Tilia americana*
Black Cherry pg. 155	*Prunus serotina*
Black Willow pg. 157	*Salix nigra*
Brown-eyed Susan pg. 165	*Rudbeckia triloba*
Common Buttonbush pg. 171	*Cephalanthus occidentalis*
Common Hackberry pg. 173	*Celtis occidentalis*
Common Hoptree pg. 175	*Ptelea trifoliata*
Eastern Redbud pg. 179	*Cercis canadensis*
Maryland Senna pg. 191	*Senna marilandica*
New Jersey Tea pg. 195	*Ceanothus americanus*
Partridge Pea pg. 203	*Chamaecrista fasciculata*
Pawpaw pg. 205	*Asimina triloba*
Pussy Willow pg. 213	*Salix discolor*
Red Maple pg. 215	*Acer rubrum*

Partial to full shade

COMMON NAME	SCIENTIFIC NAME
Cutleaf Coneflower pg. 243	*Rudbeckia laciniata*
Woodland Sunflower pg. 259	*Helianthus divaricatus*

Hummingbird Plants

Full sun

COMMON NAME	SCIENTIFIC NAME
Anise Hyssop pg. 39	*Agastache foeniculum*
Cross Vine pg. 61	*Bignonia capreolata*
Large-flowered Beardstongue, pg. 79	*Penstemon grandiflorus*
Marsh Blazing Star pg. 85	*Liatris spicata*
Meadow Blazing Star pg. 87	*Liatris ligulistylis*
Ohio Buckeye pg. 95	*Aesculus glabra*
Swamp Rosemallow pg. 131	*Hibiscus moscheutos*
Trumpet Creeper pg. 133	*Campsis radicans*
Trumpet Honeysuckle pg. 135	*Lonicera sempervirens*

Partial to full shade

COMMON NAME	SCIENTIFIC NAME
Red Columbine pg. 249	*Aquilegia canadensis*

Full sun to partial shade

COMMON NAME	SCIENTIFIC NAME
Bluebell Bellflower pg. 163	*Campanula rotundifolia*
Cardinal Flower pg. 167	*Lobelia cardinalis*
Foxglove Penstemon pg. 183	*Penstemon digitalis*
Great Blue Lobelia pg. 187	*Lobelia siphilitica*
Halberd-leaf Rosemallow, pg. 189	*Hibiscus laevis*
Michigan Lily pg. 193	*Lilium michiganense*
Obedient Plant pg. 199	*Physostegia virginiana*
Royal Catchfly pg. 217	*Silene regia*
Scarlet Bee Balm pg. 221	*Monarda didyma*
Spotted Bee Balm, pg. 223	*Monarda punctata*
White Turtlehead pg. 227	*Chelone glabra*
Wild Bergamot pg. 231	*Monarda fistulosa*

Larval Host List

If you want to attract caterpillars to your yard, these are the plants to seek out. The following plants are known larval hosts for butterflies. And as an added bonus, we've included photos of the caterpillars (when possible) and adults to help you get started on identifying any caterpillars you may find.

Monarch

Pink Swamp Milkweed, pg. 207
Asclepias incarnata

Purple Milkweed, pg. 247
Asclepias purpurascens

Showy Milkweed, pg. 117
Asclepias speciosa

Common Milkweed, pg. 53
Asclepias syriaca

Butterfly Milkweed, pg. 49
Asclepias tuberosa

Zebra Swallowtail

Pawpaw, pg. 205
Asimina triloba

Pipevine Swallowtail

Woolly Pipevine, pg. 235
Aristolochia tomentosa

Virginia Snakeroot, pg. 255
Aristolochia serpentaria

Southern Dogface

Leadplant, pg. 81
Amorpha canescens

False Indigo, pg. 181
Amorpha fruticosa

Silver-spotted Skipper

False Indigo, pg. 181
Amorpha fruticosa

Eastern Black Swallowtail

Purplestem Angelica, pg. 211
Angelica atropurpurea

Golden Alexanders, pg. 185
Zizia aurea

Red Admiral

False Nettle, pg. 245
Boehmeria cylindrica

Summer Azure
Spring Azure

New Jersey Tea, pg. 195
Ceanothus americanus

Baltimore Checkerspot

White Turtlehead, pg. 227
Chelone glabra

Little Yellow
Cloudless Sulphur
Gray Hairstreak

Partridge Pea, pg. 203
Chamaecrista fasciculata

Spicebush Swallowtail

Northern Spicebush, pg. 197
Lindera benzoin

Frosted Elfin

**Karner Blue
(federally endangered)**

Wild Lupine, pg. 233
Lupinus perennis

Gulf Fritillary

Purple Passionflower, pg. 209
Passiflora incarnata

Eastern Tiger Swallowtail

Red-spotted Purple

Coral Hairstreak

Black Cherry, pg. 155
Prunus serotina

Giant Swallowtail

Common Hoptree, pg. 175
Ptelea trifoliata

Cloudless Sulphur

Sleepy Orange

Maryland Senna, pg. 191
Senna marilandica

Viceroy

Mourning Cloak

Acadian Hairstreak

Pussy Willow, pg. 213
Salix discolor

Black Willow, pg. 157
Salix nigra

Aphrodite Fritillary

Great Spangled Fritillary

Variegated Fritillary

Meadow Fritillary

Common Blue Violet, pg. 241
Viola sororia

Northern Crescent

Pearl Crescent

Smooth Blue Aster, pg. 123
Symphyotrichum laeve

Gorgone Checkerspot

Black-eyed Susan, pg. 43
Rudbeckia hirta

Woodland Sunflower, pg. 259
Helianthus divaricatus

Northern Azure

Spring Azure

Meadowsweet, pg. 89
Spiraea alba

Cobweb Skipper

Delaware Skipper

Dusted Skipper

Big Bluestem, pg. 41
Andropogon gerardii

American Lady

Western Pearly Everlasting,
pg. 139
Anaphalis margaritacea

Cobweb Skipper

Common Wood Nymph

Crossline Skipper

Dusted Skipper

Indian Skipper

Leonard's Skipper

Swarthy Skipper

Little Bluestem, pg. 83
Schizachyrium scoparium

Southern Dogface

Reakirt's Blue

White Prairie Clover, pg. 143
Dalea candida

Southern Dogface

Purple Prairie Clover, pg. 105
Dalea purpurea

American Snout

Hackberry Emperor

Tawny Emperor

Question Mark

Mourning Cloak

Common Hackberry, pg. 173
Celtis occidentalis

RETAIL SOURCES OF MIDWEST NATIVE SEED AND PLANTS

Prairie Moon Nursery

32115 Prairie Lane
Winona, MN 55987
www.prairiemoon.com

Prairie Nursery

P.O. Box 306
Westfield, WI 53964
www.prairienursery.com

Shooting Star Native Seeds

20740 County Road 33
Spring Grove, MN 55974
www.shootingstarnativeseed.com

Roundstone Native Seed

9764 Raider Hollow Road
Upton, KY 42784
https://roundstoneseed.com

Ernst Seed

8884 Mercer Pike
Meadville, PA 16335
www.ernstseed.com

Midwest Invasive Plant Network

c/o The Morton Arboretum
4100 Illinois Route 53
Lisle, IL 60532
www.mipn.org/cwma-resources/site-revegetation/native-plant-nurseries-of-the-midwest/

If you can't find native plants near you, contact your local natural resources department, cooperative extension office, or native plant society for additional information on native plant and seed sources, native landscapers, and additional resources.

NATIVE PLANT SOCIETIES

The American Horticultural Society provides a directory of native plant societies in the U.S. and Canada: www.ahsgardening.org/gardening-resources/societies-clubs-organizations /native-plant-societies

COOPERATIVE EXTENSION SERVICE

Nearly every county in the U.S. has an extension office, where experts from state universities provide scientific knowledge and expertise to the public on various topics, including natural resources, agriculture, and horticulture. They are often excellent resources for gardeners and those planning a native garden. The National Pesticide Information Center maintains an interactive directory of extension offices across the country at: http://npic.orst.edu/pest/countyext.htm

BOTANICAL GARDENS AND ARBORETUMS

The American Horticultural Society maintains an interactive directory of U.S. botanical gardens and arboretums, which is searchable by zip code at: www.ahsgardening.org/gardening-programs /rap/the-garden-guide

Images used under license from shutterstock.com. Some photos identified by page in a left (ex. L1) to right (ex. R1) order, descending.

53931: 160; **A.Bulano:** 26 (R4); **A.G.A:** 19 (top 1); **Vahan Abrahamyan:** 24 (L9), 32 (L4), 220, 261 (18); **aDam Wildlife:** 21 (top 4); **Erik Agar:** 30 (R1), 169; **ahmydaria:** 125; **AJCespedes:** 9; **ajt:** 20 (top 3); **Scisetti Alfio:** 264 (bottom left); **Arty Alison:** 30 (L3), 150 (Common Buttonbush), 170, 174; **alybaba:** 30 (L9), 260 (7); **AnaGoncalves93:** 272 (American Lady larva); **John A. Anderson:** 197; **APugach:** 28 (L11); **arousa:** 153; **ASakoulis:** 21 (top 2); **Nina B:** 116; **Lana B:** 200, 263 (9); **Dan Bagur:** 270 (Red Admiral larva); **Mark Baldwin:** 26 (L1), 26 (R9), 114, 261 (15), 262 (3); **Bonnie Taylor Barry:** 271 (Pearl Crescent); **Jim Beers:** 135; **Gabriela Beres:** 28 (L1), 122; **Erin Bergman:** 157; **beverlyjane:** 83; **Robert Biedermann:** 28 (L10); **Gerry Bishop:** 24 (R6), 26 (L3), 26 (L4), 28 (L4), 28 (L7), 30 (R5), 30 (L11), 32 (L9), 60, 88, 92, 146, 223, 261 (13), 262 (2), 263 (8); Randy Bjorklund:), 270 (Pipevine Swallowtail), 272 (American Snout); **bjphotographs:** 80, 81; **Karel Bock:** 21 (bottom 3); **Artur Bogacki:** 32 (R9); **Stephen Bonk:** 28 (R1); **Jennifer Bosvert:** 19 (top 6), 93; **Arlen E Breiholz:** 30 (R6), 188; **SJ Brown:** 228, 262 (6); **Jen Burrows:** 37 (Big Bluestem); **Steve Byland:** 231, 259; **c_WaldWiese:** 30 (L7), 190, 260 (1); **Julianne Caust:** 37 (Black-eyed Susan), 42; **ChWeiss:** 26 (R8), 110, 204; **Kathy Clark:** 24 (R8), 32 (R3), 68, 218, 263 (10); **Charles Collard:** 134; **Kevin Collison:** 217; **COULANGES:** 38, 262 (7), 264 (1); **Cryptographer:** 24 (R1); **Joan D G:** 69; **damann:** 24 (L4), 261 (4); **Dan4Earth:** 12, 24 (L3), 46; **Judy M Darby:** 44; **Sharon Day:** 28 (R7), 36 (Indian Blanket), 74, 263 (18), 264 (2); **Peter de Kievith:** 266 bottom; **Danita Delmont:** 20 (top 1), 95, 103, 147, 270 (Baltimore Checkerspot); **Courtney A Denning:** 26 (L8), 109; **Marjan Despotovic:** 133; **Bruce Dierenfield:** 151 (Purple Passionflower), 208; **Digieva:** 102, 265 (4); **dlamb302:** 26 (R3), 91; **Alla Dmitrijeva:** 266 middle; **Le Do:** 32 (L6); **Dennis W Donohue:** 271 (Great Spangled Fritillary); **Pat Dooley:** 271 (Viceroy); **HK Dougherty:** 201, 262 (bottom left); **EQRoy:** 30 (R10); **Hank Erdmann:** 124; **Amy Estoye:** 272 (Swarthy Skipper); **Evalie:** 121; **Melinda Fawver:** 32 (R8), 171, 236 (Purple Milkweed), 240; **Shannon Marie Ferguson:** 253; **Sheila Fitzgerald:** 26 (L9), 112; **Flower_Garden:** 28 (L2); **Dmitry Fokin:** 54; **FotoRequest:** 1; **Tyler Fox:** 271 (Giant Swallowtail larva); **Gus Garcia:** 127; **gardenlife:** 65, 183; **Luchia Georganta:** 270 (Karner Blue); **Linda George:** 32 (L11), 237 (Sweet Joe Pye Weed), 250, 261 (10); **Bob Grabowski:** 237 (Red Columbine), 248; **Anna Gratys:** 34 (L2); **Jerrold James Griffith:** 86; **guentermanaus:** 150 (Foxglove Penstemon), 182, 261 (14); **Gunsmith Photos:** 24 (L7), 63; **Arto Hakola:** 270 (Spicebush Swallowtail); **Michael E Hall:** 131; **Alison Hancock:** 10; **Elliotte Rusty Harold:** 19 (top 3), 21 (middle 1, middle 2), 41, 270 (Spring Azure), 271 (Spring Azure); **Cameron M Hartley:** 272 (Crossline Skipper); **Hecos:** 77; **Jon E Heintz Jr:** 167; **Shawn Hempel:** 270 (Cloudless Sulphur), 271 (Cloudless Sulphur); **High Mountain:** 30 (R9); **HilaryH:** 161; **Jeff Holcombe:** 32 (R2), 47, 53; **Catherine M Hollander:** 30 (R3); **Brett Hondow:** 271 (Pearl Crescent larva), 272 (Tawny Emperor larva); **Karyn Honor:** 98; **ileana_bt:** 28 (L3); **Vitaly Ilyasov:** 59; **InfoFlowersPlants:** 26 (L11), 48, 120, 263 (16, 20); **islavicek:** 28 (R6), 30 (R2), 34-35, 172; **Malachi Jacobs:** 20 (middle 1); **Frode Jacobsen:** 272 (Dusted Skipper, Question Mark); **Jukka Jantunen:** 271 (Northern Azure); **Matt Jeppson:** 271 (Eastern Tiger Swallowtail larva); **Jillian Cain Photography:** 270 (Cloudless Sulphur larva), 271 (Cloudless Sulphur larva); **Yuttana Joe:** 19 (top 4); **rushka johnson:** 13; **JPL Designs:** 55; **Rob Jump:** 30 (L4), 179; **JurateBuiviene:** 24 (L1), 261 (16); **Sirle Kabanen:** 28 (L5), 138; **Kamrad71:** 24 (R10), 265 (5); **David Byron Keener:** 15, 99, 272 (Question Mark larva); **Cathy Keifer:** 149, 270 (Monarch larva); **Kenneth Keifer:** 32 (L1), 34 (L1), 237 (Virginia Bluebells), 247, 252, 261 (8); **Hway Kiong Kim:** 19 (bottom 4); **Jeff Kingma:** 272 (Leonard's Skipper); **sharon kingston:** 6; **Tomasz Klejdsz:** 14; **Serguei Koultchitskii:** 271 (Giant Swallowtail); **Jon Kraft:** 94, 205; **kukuruxa:** 24 (L6); **Jitender kumarj:** 272 (Indian Skipper); **Nikolay Kurzenko:** 260 (2); **kzww:** 18; **Guste L:** 39; **Brian Lasenby:** 45, 193, 241, 249, 271 (Coral Hairstreak); **Olivier Le Queinec:** 266 top; **Doug Lemke:** 20 (middle 2), 159, 272 (Tawny Emperor); **Peter F. Lenehan:** 30 (R7); **LianeM:** 15; **Jerry Lin:** 36 (Marsh Blazing Star), 84; **littlewormy:** 26 (L2), 261 (19); **Svetlana Mahovskaya:** 30 (L8), 194; **MainlightPhoto.com:** 216; **Kazakov Maksim:** 76; **marich:** 28 (R5), 140; **Marinodenisenko:** 164; **markh:** 21 (top 3); **Vladimir Martinov:** 28 (L8), 152; **Lipatova Maryna:** 175, 181; **MashimaraPhoto:** 70; **Kateryna Mashkevych:** 212; **Dave Massey:** 213; **M. McGann:** 19 (bottom 1), 49; **McGraw:** 261 (9); **Michael G McKinne:** 26 (R1), 82, 260 (6), 271 (Variegated Fritillary); **Media Marketing:** 206, 207; **meiningi:** 28 (R10); **melissamn:** 236 (Woodland Sunflower), 258; **meunierd:** 26 (R6), 268; **Marek Mierzejewski:** 150 (Michigan Lily), 192; **Miles28:** 270 (Spicebush Swallowtail larva); **MilsiArt:** 177; **Young Swee Ming:** 272 (Delaware Skipper); **Ravshan Mirzaitov:** 271 (Mourning Cloak), 272 (Mourning Cloak); **Mitotico:** 21 (bottom 1); **mizy:** 30 (R8), 36 (Cup Plant), 64, 90, 186, 196, 262 (1); **David S Mohn:** 24 (R9), 36 (Horay Vervain), 72; **Przemyslaw Muszynski:** 28 (R8), 154; **ncristian:** 151 (Eastern Prickly Pear), 176; **Marty Nelson:** 26 (L10); **B V Nickel:** 24 (L2), 261 (17); **Nico Muller Art:** 233; **Nadezda Nikitina:** 32 (L2); **nnattalli:** 30 (R4); **Michael Sean O'Leary:** 221; **Steven Russell Smith Ohio:** 19 (bottom 2), 272 (Common Wood Nymph); **Alan Olander:** 26 (R2), 87; **Nancy J. Ondra:** 106, 184; **Jay Ondreicka:** 219, 270 (Eastern Black Swallowtail larva); **Sari ONeal:** 32 (R7), 43, 234, 235, 271 (Gulf Fritillary larva), 271 (Gulf Fritillary), 271 (Eastern Tiger Swallowtail), 271 (Sleepy Orange), 271 (Viceroy larva), 271 (Variegated Fritillary larva), 271 (Gorgone Checkerspot larva), 271 (Gorgone Checkerspot), 272 (Gorgone Checkerspot larva), 272 (Gorgone Checkerspot), 272 (Reakirt's Blue); **OrelImages:** 30 (L10), 202; **Massimiliano Paolino:** 271 (Mourning Cloak larva), 272 (Mourning Cloak larva); **Michelle Patrick:** 32 (L10); **Paul Reeves Photography:** 19 (top 2), 20 (top 4), 20 (middle 3), 21 (middle 3, middle 4), 21 (middle 4), 24 (R7), 270 (Baltimore Checkerspot larva), 271 (Northern Crescent); **alan payne:** 21 (top 5); **Peter Turner Photography:** 96, 261 (11), 265 (3); **Peyker:** 126; **Polarpx:** 26 (L5); **Luc Pouliot:** 19 (top 5); **David Prahl:** 8; **prambuwesas:** 163; **Randy R:** 272 (Common Hackberry); **Andy Reago & Chrissy McClarren:** 203; **redclovestudio:** 20 (top 2); **Daniel Reiner:** 28 (R3), 132; **Steph Reuse:** 32 (R5), 226; **Leena Robinson:** 260 (Common Buckeye), 272 (American Lady); **Marina Rose:** 123; **Jason Patrick Ross:** 24 (R3); **Manfred Ruckszio:** 32 (R6), 230, 261 (12); **RukiMedia:** 24 (L8), 26 (R7), 30 (L6), 66, 107; **Ioana Rut:** 198; **Mariola Anna S:** 24 (R4), 52, 263 (15); **Andrew Sabai:** 28 (R2), 129, 263 (11); **SariMe:** 151 (Bluebell Bellflower), 162, 263 (13); **Michael Schober:** 117; **Ole Schoener:** 32 (R4), 37 (Common Ironweed), 50, 51, 97, 222, 263 (19); **Ken Schulze:** 62, 261 (5); **M. Schuppich:** 85; **Kyle Selcer:** 257; **Annette Shaff:** 21 (bottom 5); **Michael Shake:** 32 (L7), 232; **Cynthia Shirk:** 151 (Red Maple), 214; **marc sims:** 267 (top left); **Gurcharan Singh:** 255; **Scott F Smith:** 272 (Cobweb Skipper); **Richard G Smith:** 75; **Sue Smith:** 32 (R10); **Sokor Space:** 24 (L5), 37 (Common Ninebark); **Paul Sparks:** 271 (Acadian Hairstreak); **Angelchev Sprydon:** 24 (L10); **Josef Stemeseder:** 270 (Eastern Black Swallowtail), 271 (Red-spotted Purple), 271 (Meadow Fritillary); **steve52:** 19 (bottom 6); **Susan Marie Sullivan:** 26 (L6), 37 (Prairie Dock), 100; **Sunbunny Studio:** 58, 263 (17); **Krista Marie T:** 26 (L7), 105; **T-I:** 104, 187, 263 (12); **tanakomsar:** 6; **Tathoms:** 251, 274; **TechnoSavage:** 271 (Red-spotted Purple larva); **mccw thissen:** 26 (R5); **Cheryl Thomas:** 270 (Monarch); **Gabor Tinz:** 267 (middle); **Tippy Tortue:** 32 (R1), 210, 211; **tlindsayg:** 137; 260 (3); **tome213:** 24 (R2); **tribp:** 67; **Tunatura:** 57; **Iva Vagnerova:** 24 (L11), 56, 78, 263 (14); **Johan van Beilen:** 21 (top 1); **Vanessa Vial:** 189; **Iva Villi:** 24 (R5), 30 (L5), 236 (Cutleaf Coneflower), 242; **Jaco Visser:** 21 (bottom 2); **Marek Walica:** 11, 23; **Jim and Lynne Weber:** 270 (Southern Dogface), 272 (Southern Dogface); **J Wheeler:** 32 (L3); **Olga Yudina:** 150 (Eastern Redbud), 178; **Abeselom Zerit:** 271 (Aphrodite Fritillary); **zzz555zzz:** 158.

About the Author

Jaret C. Daniels, Ph.D., is a professional nature photographer, author, native plant enthusiast, and entomologist at the University of Florida, specializing in insect ecology and conservation. He has authored numerous scientific papers, popular articles, and books on gardening, wildlife conservation, insects, and butterflies, including butterfly field guides for Florida, Georgia, the Carolinas, Ohio, and Michigan. He is also coauthor of *Wildflowers of Florida Field Guide* and *Wildflowers of the Southeast Field Guide*. Jaret currently lives in Gainesville, Florida, with his wife, Stephanie.